D0818879

I Hate Myself and Want to Die

I Hate Myself and Want to Die

THE 52 MOST DEPRESSING SONGS YOU'VE EVER HEARD

TOM REYNOLDS

HYPERION

New York

Copyright © Tom Reynolds, 2006

Illustrations by Stacey Earley

A previous edition of this book was published in Great Britain by Sanctuary
Publishing in 2005.
Cover design: Ash
Author photo: Denise Bellingham

Selection of lyrics from "Gloomy Sunday"
Original Words by Laszlo Javor
English Translation by Desmond Carter and Sam Lewis
Music by Rezsoe Seress
© 1936 Csardas-Zenemuekiado and Editio Musica Budapest Music Publisher Ltd,
Hungary
(93.75%) Warner/Chappell Music Ltd, London W6 8BS
(6.25%) Redwood Music Ltd, London NW1 8BD
Lyrics reproduced by permission of IMP Ltd
All Rights Reserved.

All rights reserved. No part of this book may be used or reproduced in any manner
whatsoever without the written permission of the Publisher. Printed in the United
States of America. For information address Hyperion, 77 West 66th Street, New York,
New York 10023-6298.

Library of Congress Cataloging-in-Publication Data

Reynolds, Tom.
  I hate myself and want to die : the 52 most depressing songs you've ever heard /
Tom Reynolds.
    p. cm.
   ISBN 1-4013-0835-X
    1. Popular music—Humor. 2. Sadness in music—Humor. I. Title.
  ML65 .R653 2006   2006041108

Hyperion books are available for special promotions and premiums. For details
contact Michael Rentas, Assistant Director, Inventory Operations, Hyperion,
77 West 66th Street, 12th floor, New York, New York 10023, or call 212-456-0133.

FIRST EDITION

10 9 8 7 6 5 4 3 2 1

Contents

I Hate Myself and Want to Die

The Anatomy of Melancholy
or A Brief History of the Depressing Song

MY FIRST experience with depressing music came when I was very young, courtesy of my parents. They owned without question the most radical set of albums ever gathered within a suburban household. No, it wasn't Switched-on Bach, Captain Beefheart, or the collected works of Karlheinz Stockhausen—I'm talking about the really weird stuff: Mantovani, 101 Strings, Ferrante and Teicher, Andre Kostelantz, The New Cristy Minstrels, and Herb Alpert And The Tijuana Brass. Today's neo-hipsters refer to these acts as "vintage lounge," but they were really the Greatest Generation's contribution to psychedelia. Never mind the Grateful Dead, try to sit through a *Sing Along with Mitch Miller* album without wondering who spiked the Kool-Aid. I spent much of my single-digit years staring bemused at the manhole-sized woofers of my dad's speakers while a sing-and-hum choir eviscerated a song I'd never heard before but readily sensed was being butchered all the same. It was unsettling enough to make me spin my brother's 45-rpm single of The Royal Guardsmen's "Snoopy and the Red Baron" just to kick out the jams.

It wasn't until Christmas that the despair really hit.

The yuletide season brought out the familial DJ in my parents, and they would spin every Christmas album they had in their ample collection. I heard The New Cristy Minstrels' demented banjo-driven version of "Do You Hear What I Hear," Mario Lanza throwing his tonsils into "O Holy Night" like a

Tuscan auctioneer, Julie Andrews cooing her way through "I Saw Three Ships" in that chanteuse style of hers that sounded like she dined on clouds. Inevitably, though, I had to endure the one song that sent me into a spiraling despair that rivaled Hemingway's just before he reached for the 12-gauge: "What Child Is This?"

I know it's a beloved Christmas carol but, truth be told, "What Child Is This?" depressed the crap out of me. Renaissance music authorities will know it as "Greensleeves," and its melody is built on the most depressing scale in music: the Dorian mode (for neophytes, the Dorian mode is D to d on the white keys of the piano; noodle around with it for ten minutes, and you'll be tying nooses in your head). Most of the aforementioned artists included "What Child Is This?" on their respective Christmas albums, so I was treated to no less than nine different versions of it. The most debilitating for me was Ray Coniff's arrangement for orchestra and choir; it sounded like nothing short of four dozen zombies out on a midnight prowl for brains. Hearing an undead chorus of male voices moaning "*Whaatt chiilld is thiiisss who's laaaiid to ressstt*" sent me into a serious crying bout in my bedroom every time. To this day, I cannot hear "What Child Is This?" without envisioning a pillow covered with snot.

Since then, my depressing music tastes have expanded dramatically. There are currently scores of songs that never fail to burrow into my brain and screw with my serotonin levels. All of them will clear the dance floor at a rave and some will send K-Mart shoppers running for the gun counter to make a speedy purchase. I cherish most depressing songs the way I do a root canal treatment: something I don't want to remember, but am unable to forget.

OF COURSE, I'm not the first to feel this way. The genesis of the depressing song dates back to ancient times, when poets started putting their verses to music. This was a dubious decision because poets are very miserable people. They have no money, dress badly, and their families think they should get a real job. The first depressing songster of note was probably Homer, the blind poet and lyre player who groped his way around the Greek Isles in 700 BC, bumping into statues of Athena while performing wherever he could book a gig. Refusing to sing covers, Homer only did original material, and his entire repertoire consisted of two songs: *The Iliad* and *The Odyssey*. Each took three full days to perform. A typical Homer concert was by itself depressing: a wizened old man hunched over a tiny harp braying on about Hector and Patroclus while angry audiences screamed requests and pelted him with week-old hummus. Blind and impatient, Homer never wrote down anything, so his lyrics varied weekly, depending on his mood. Some versions of *The Iliad* ended with the Trojans torching the wooden horse, incinerating the Greeks inside while inventing the first post-war barbecue. Others had Helen infecting the Castle Troy archers with the clap while Achilles is castrated following a catapult malfunction. Listeners were flung into pits of despair, prompting the occasional suicide attempt through mass ingestion of pimentos.

Over the centuries, verses were condensed and the first songs of note came to fruition in the form of the "Ballade." Many traditional Scottish/English ballads of the Renaissance are still some of the most horrific tunes ever conceived. This is because the actual Renaissance in no way resembled today's Renaissance fairs. Nobody took Visa, and the average person didn't live past twenty seven; it was an entire planet of *Real World* cast members. You either died of plague or were burned alive for being a witch. Such inauspicious circumstances gave rise to the murder ballad. Here's a sampling from the traditional fifteenth-century song "Edward," in which the title character enters the family castle covered with blood right after chopping up his dad. His mother asks:

"Why dois your sword so drip with blood,
Edward, Edward,
Why dois your sword so drip with blood,
And why so glad, my son?"

"O I have killed my hawk so good,
Mother, mother,
O I have killed my hawk so good."

"Your hawk's blood was never so red,
Edward, Edward,
Your hawk's blood was never so red,
My dear son, I tell thee."

"O I have killed my father dear,
Mother, mother,
O I have killed my father dear."

What a brat.

Over time, trained composers jumped on the grim bandwagon and returned depressing music to its Homeric roots via long-form works. Opera became the established medium, utilizing plotlines so tragic they made Hamlet look like an episode of *SpongeBob SquarePants*. You had to sit for hours wanting to kill yourself as characters were buried alive, decapitated, poisoned, dragged off to Hell or, in the case of the heroine of *La Bohème*, forced to die slowly from consumption, coughing up blood while nailing four octaves the entire time. Audiences filed out emotionally wrung dry and returned home to smelling salts and a hearty glass of laudanum.

Standard songwriting, on the other hand, had long fallen behind the curve, particularly in America where the only people composing depressing tunes were the Indians, curiously ungrateful about losing their land and seeing their bison obliterated. Tunesmiths like Stephen Foster composed bright, catchy ditties about rivers and horse racing. Everyone was happy in a Foster song, even the "darkies" forced to do all the heavy lifting.* Songwriters discovered how well words like moon, croon, and June rhymed. Barbershop quartets appeared on street corners like crime families, harmonizing cheerfully about the alma mater and girls named Rose. By the twentieth century, Tin Pan Alley composers like George and Ira Gershwin, Cole Porter, Harold Arlen, Rodgers and Hart, and Frank Loesser were cranking out hundreds of musical gems, not one of them a truly depressing song. Sad maybe, but not depressing. (I know, some of you are thinking, "What about blues music?" Trust me; the black artists who wrote and sang the blues weren't depressed, they were pissed off.)

It took the more somber Europeans to pick up the slack, likely from having to host two world wars with no security deposit to cover the cleanup. The legendary French singer Edith Piaf, aka the Little Sparrow, had all of Paris in a weepy swoon with her tragic songs about unrequited love and broken hearts. Though mostly remembered for "La Vie En Rose," my personal favorite of hers for sheer depression is "Bravo Pour Le Clown," which is about a sad clown who goes lunatic because he never heard a "Bravo!" that wasn't laced with sarcasm. In a 1956 concert at New York's Carnegie Hall, Piaf tells the audience in broken English how the clown heard " 'bravo' from his unfaithful wife, 'bravo' from his children who hate him. Suddenly, realizing all his grief, he kills his wife. Since then, [he's] locked up in an asylum. In his madness, he hears a 'bravo!' he missed all his life . . ." The accordions kick in and the audience revels in a French-language clown murder song.

Probably the most notorious depressing song of the pre–World War II era is 1933's "Gloomy Sunday," also known as

---

* Foster himself was a depressive dipsomaniac.

the "Hungarian Suicide Song." As the story goes, "Gloomy Sunday" is allegedly so depressing it's driven people to commit suicide after just one listen. (Personally, I can think of any number of Ashlee Simpson songs that have the same effect, but for entirely different reasons.) The music and original lyrics of "Gloomy Sunday" were the creation of Rezsô Seress, a pianist and composer born in Hungary in 1899. After being dumped by his fiancée for being a failure, Seress supposedly sat down and wrote a bitter tune about how he felt. The first stanza goes like this:

> *Ôsz van és peregnek a sárgult levelek*
> *Meghalt a földön az emberi szerete*
> *Bánatos könnyekkel zokog az öszi szél*
> *Szívem már új tavaszt nem vár és nem remél*
> *Hiába sírok és hiába szenvedek*
> *Szívtelen rosszak és kapzsik az emberek . . .*

Though my Hungarian's a little rusty, this translates to something like this:

> I can't believe you dumped me,
> You ungrateful little she-whore.

Seress got "Gloomy Sunday" published, and it became a popular melancholy hit, a sort of Hungarian "Feelings." Flushed with his first success, Seress tried to reconcile with his fiancée and sent her the lyrics in lieu of flowers. The next day, she killed herself. After that, strange things began to happen.

In February of 1936, Budapest Police were investigating the suicide of a local shoemaker, Joseph Keller. The investigation showed that Keller had left a suicide note in which he quoted the lyrics of a recent popular song. The song was "Gloomy Sunday."

Following this event, seventeen additional people took their own lives. In each case, "Gloomy Sunday" was closely connected with the circumstances surrounding the suicide.[*]

The "Gloomy Sunday" suicide curse falls into chicken-or-egg country: Did the song drive people to kill themselves, or was it simply used as a punctuation mark by people who were planning on punching out early anyway? Legend has it that dozens of suicides were found with the lyrics to "Gloomy Sunday" near their dead bodies and that the Hungarian government banned the song as being too depressing.

English versions of "Gloomy Sunday" were done by the lyricists Sam M. Lewis and Desmond Carter, each of whom penned their own translations of the lyrics. The Lewis version, recorded by Hal Kemp and His Orchestra, with Bob Allen on vocals, became a hit in America in 1936:

> Sunday is gloomy, my hours are slumberless
> Dearest the shadows I live with are numberless
> Little white flowers will never awaken you
> Not where the black coach of sorrow has taken you
> Angels have no thought of ever returning you
> Would they be angry if I thought of joining you?

Supposedly, both the BBC and American radio stations banned English-language versions of "Gloomy Sunday" from airplay in order to offset the body count, though this claim is hard to verify. There is one confirmed report of a New York typist committing suicide by gassing herself and leaving behind a note requesting that "Gloomy Sunday" be played at her funeral. There are currently more than a hundred suicides attributed to

---

[*] From a Web site of dubious scholarship.

"Gloomy Sunday," though, again, postmortems cannot confirm this ("Cause of death: song written by a Hungarian").

"Gloomy Sunday" has grown so much in urban-legend status that there is even a 1999 German film about its cursed notoriety, entitled *Ein Lied von Liebe und Tod*. It should be noted, however, that more than 150 different artists have recorded "Gloomy Sunday," and none of them committed suicide as a result of the experience, although Seress himself, in a sobering coda to the story, jumped to his death from his flat in 1968. The most popular version of the song remains Billie Holiday's 1941 recording and yes, it's a bleak mother (though not as grim as "Strange Fruit," which is included in this book).

THE GOLDEN era of the depressing song did not come about until after World War II and the advent of rock 'n' roll. As the 1960s got up to speed, numerous disturbing aspects were introduced to everyday life: assassinations, missile crises, Vietnam, riots, Charles Manson, and the twenty-minute drum solo. Reacting to how lousy everything seemed, more and more songwriters created downbeat songs about politics, war, and ungrateful wenches who ditched them for someone with more money. They noticed that music critics were heaping praises on Bob Dylan, the sulking folkie who wrote indecipherable tunes and croaked them out in an adenoidal voice. This became a crucial part of the template for the musical artiste, and performers finally understood it—in order for critics to take you seriously, you had to follow a specific formula:

1. Write a song with really depressing lyrics.
2. Sing it with a shitty voice.

To this day, musicians like Leonard Cohen, John Prine, Tom Waits, Patti Smith, Bruce Springsteen, Tom Petty, and Steve Earle are critical favorites because they're blessed with really crappy voices. It became de rigueur for singers to record a tortured song with downer lyrics to prove that they were "serious" artists. Some succeeded, while many others—including several of those named above—produced works that remain limb-gnawing masterpieces of melodic misery.

ALL OF this makes the task at hand very difficult. In selecting fifty-two of the most depressing songs ever recorded, where do you start?

Definitions help. There is a common misconception that sad songs and depressing songs are the same thing. They're not, though most are meant to be the former and end up as the latter. No one sets out to purposely write a depressing song, except for hardcore death metal acts that are so nihilistic, they defeat their own purpose and end up sounding silly. It's the musical artists with noble intentions who are behind classic depressing songs. The concept of "less is more" is tossed aside in favor of horrible lyrics, pretentious production, and an overwrought vocal performance straight out of the school of caterwaul. In short, sad songs offer the listener empathetic comfort, reflection, and wisdom. Depressing songs just make you want to stick a Glock-9 in your mouth.

Depressing songs don't always need overtly depressing lyrics (although this helps), since the horror can come from various musical missteps that further enflame the inferno. One of the most egregious is the brain concussion modulation, or BCM. This is when vocalists, anxious to show that they can hit a high J, wait breathlessly while the orchestra slams the music into a higher key. BCMs are found near the end of practically every 1990s power love ballad sung by the Big Three: Celine Dion, Mariah Carey, and Whitney Houston.

Another depressing aspect is a song's length, which triggers the Rasputin Effect[*]: Right when you think the song is over and dead, it comes back to torment you further. Several songs listed in this book run seven minutes or more in duration, as if the performer wanted to lay down an extra layer of napalm to make sure nobody survived.

The most important factor to depressing songs is their ubiquity. While many classics are one-hit wonders that killed the careers of their performers in the process, others come from established popular artists. The latter are the most lethal, because there's a good chance you're going to keep hearing the damned things on the radio.

In the end, depressing songs rattle your spirit for a variety of reasons, so the fifty-two titles in this book are grouped together into ten different genres, as follows.

I Was a Teenage Car Crash collects songs about selfless (and shockingly stupid) adolescents who sacrifice themselves so they can die for someone whose school locker just happens to be next to theirs.

I Hate Myself and Want to Die gathers together self-pitying songs in which the singer is under the delusion that his or her personal problems are of great interest to everyone.

Pretentious songs where excessive blather is mistaken for wisdom and sensitivity are found in the category of *I'm Trying to Be Profound and Touching, But Really Suck at It.*

If I Sing About Drugs, People Will Take Me Seriously: "I'm jamming a needle into my arm! Lemme tell you allllll about it!!"

In *She Hates Me, I Hate Her*, a couple's crumbling relationship is put to music, then dumped on listeners, who are expected to act as unpaid therapists.

For *Horrifying Remakes of Already Depressing Songs*, a

---

[*] Named for the Russian mystic from the court of Czar Nicholas II, who survived five assassination attempts.

mildly gloomy tune is transformed into a thing of utter horror. Think Mary Shelley's *Frankenstein* with a rhythm section.

Narrative songs based on the kind of babble you hear from the drunk guy next to you at a bar who won't shut up are collected under the banner *I'm Telling a Story Nobody Wants to Hear*.

I Had No Idea That Song Was So Morbid: the most deceptive of depressing songs, these camouflage unbelievably depressing lyrics under upbeat happy music.

A depressing song Hall of Fame, *I Mope, Therefore I Am* collects songs by artists who've built their entire careers on bumming the shit out of everyone.

Finally, *Perfect Storms*: the absolute most depressing.

Only a handful of tunes qualify as "perfect storms," where numerous factors unite to create a depressing song of live-wolverine-shoved-down-my-pants proportions. Perfect storms occur when songwriters, attempting to create an emotionally affecting song, swing for the catharsis fence but end up fouling into the grandstand, wiping out 1,000 nuns and orphans. There's an inherent cluelessness to perfect storms, with the perpetrator completely unaware of the catastrophe that's been unleashed. They're the audio equivalent of a Donner Party guide loudly insisting he knows the way through the pass.

How fitting that the worst of them is a Christmas song.

I Was a

Teenage

Car Crash

Tell Laura I Love Her

Performed by Ray Peterson
Released 1960 (No. 1 in the US)
Performed by Ricky Valance
Released 1960 (No. 1 in the UK)
Written by Jeff Barry and Ben Raleigh

STORIES OF teenagers prematurely shuffling off their mortal coils have been around since *Romeo and Juliet* and the rise of American car culture during the 1950s and early 1960s inspired the dispiriting Teenage Car Crash songs. These involve a young couple who is madly in love until one of them perishes in a fiery car wreck, leaving the other alone to grieve. These are noble fatalities, mind you, none of them ever involving booze, drugs, or carjacking. The young protagonists of TCC songs die because of selfless love and a preternatural lack of any brains whatsoever.

"Tell Laura I Love Her" was the first major TCC song—a weepy ballad about a love-struck teenage boy named Tommy who ends up getting cremated on a racetrack for the love of his girlfriend, Laura. The song was originally a number-one hit in the US for Ray Peterson in early 1960, while a cover version by Welsh singer Ricky Valance went to the top of the UK charts the same year. It's important to point out that at the time, rock 'n' roll in general sucked like a galaxy-devouring black hole. "Tell Laura" would be both Peterson's and Valance's only hit, forever cursing them both to sing it throughout their careers.

The Song

Both Peterson's and Valance's versions of "Tell Laura I Love

Her" rely on an arpeggiating guitar figure that could be found on 98 percent of the songs released back then. Early rock 'n' roll fans will recognize it instantly as will zygotes that were conceived last week. We learn about Tommy and Laura: young, white, and looking forward to their future together in Kennedy's America. They would fit easily into the comic strip *Archie* as bit players, looking on nonplussed while Betty and Veronica got into a catfight. Tommy is especially gaga about his Laura and wants to buy her an engagement ring but, alas, doesn't have the money to buy it. That's when he sees a poster advertising a stock car race with a first prize of $1,000. *That's the ticket,* Tommy tells himself. *I'll enter the race, compete in a sport I know nothing about, and come in first so that I'll win the thousand dollars.* Ah, good plan.

Naturally, this enterprising epiphany only serves to foreshadow the tragedy that follows. Once we hear "he saw a sign for a stock car race," we already know Tommy's a few hours away from being turned into a briquette. Flushed with excitement, Tommy hurriedly calls Laura. She isn't home so the doomed lad leaves a message with her mother: "Tell Laura I love her, tell Laura I need her, tell Laura I may be late, I've something to do that cannot wait."

Tommy's message sets off the tragic sequence of events that follow, just as in *Romeo and Juliet* when Romeo fails to receive word that Juliet is only faking her death. (I'm comparing this song with Shakespeare because, well, it makes me laugh.) Tommy is the youngest driver at the track, of course, the others being old geezers in their mid-twenties. Rather than send him home with a gentle scolding, the race officials allow him to compete while stifling their laughter. I'm not well-versed in NASCAR rules but I'm fairly certain they frown on high-school boys showing up in boxy Chevys with bald tires and faulty clutches. Besides, Tommy has no pit crew and is completely clueless as to the basic strategies of auto racing (i.e., slamming into a wall is generally not a good idea). Within a few laps he rolls the car, which becomes engulfed in flames. He is pulled out of the wreckage, coughing up carbon before proclaiming his love for Laura and uttering with his last breath: "Tell Laura not to cry, my love for her will never die . . ." By the last stanza, Laura is alone in the church, praying for her Tommy. In the chapel's echo-filled acoustics, she can still hear his haunting cries of how he still loves her (and it's just as creepy as it sounds).

Why It's Depressing

At the time "Tell Laura" was released, Elvis had been drafted, Buddy Holly, Richie Valens, and the Big Bopper were dead, and Eddie Cochran soon would be. The airwaves were ruled by lame teen idols like Tommy Sands and Fabian, and both Ray Peterson and Ricky Valance fit right in with all the Anglo blandness. Peterson was originally a rockabilly singer but, after noticing how Gene Vincent and the Burnette Brothers hadn't made a dime singing rockabilly, went the pop route and hit number one with the tragic "Tell Laura I Love Her." Neither Peterson nor Valance are bad crooners, but both practically sob "Tell Laura" with an articulation that's so pronounced they sound like Eliza Doolittle practicing "The Rain in Spain."

Like all TCC songs, "Tell Laura" is a relic from a time long vanished. Today's teenagers eat it in car wrecks while reaching for their cell phones or go driving off a cliff leaving an outdoor rave. As for $1,000, it's going toward a laptop or his-and-hers iPods. In retrospect, the song is more about futility than sacrifice. True, Tommy dies for his Laura but, let's face it, if he had survived and won the race, he'd be unbearable. Tommy getting scorched on the track saved Laura from a future with a reckless idiot who thinks every one of his harebrained ideas is a sure-fire winner. Nine years into their doomed marriage, Laura, seven months pregnant with their third child, would be rolling her eyes as Tommy, bankrupt from his third business venture, stands in the backyard by the barbecue regaling the neighbors with the story of his race track victory for the hundred and forty-third time. Later, during the trial separation, Tommy would be sulking at the Dew Drop Inn downing Pabst Blue Ribbon and whining to the bartender, "Can you believe she threw me out? I won a stock car race for her. Hey, did I ever tell you that story? See, what happened was, I saw this sign . . ." Good riddance.

Teen Angel

Performed by Mark Dinning
Released 1960
(No. 37 in the UK, although it was banned, no. 1 in the US)
Written by Jean Dinning

RELEASED IN January 1960, the inane "Teen Angel" followed closely on the heels of "Tell Laura I Love Her" and stayed faithful to the TCC template: The victim sacrifices herself to demonstrate her eternal love for her boyfriend. In other words, she dies from an appalling lack of common sense for which she is not called to task later during the memorial ("We are gathered here today to remember the Teen Angel who passed away because she had the brains of a fly . . ."). The song ups the tragedy level of "Tell Laura" a few degrees by giving the adolescent girl a chance to escape her grim fate. Alas, the Teen Angel makes a fatal decision that leads to her getting flattened in front of her boyfriend's eyes.

Though "Teen Angel" has been a campy staple of Sha Na Na's live show for decades, the original version was sung by a warbling tenor named Mark Dinning, whose three older siblings comprised the Dinning Sisters, a vocal act from the 1940s who charted a few minor hits. Mark followed in their footsteps and made a futile attempt at being a rock 'n' roller, which he clearly wasn't. Sister Jean Dinning helped out her little brother by penning the white-bread "Teen Angel" for him, and his recording of it for MGM went to number one. In retrospect, Dinning was the ultimate good soldier just following orders: "Rip off Ray Peterson? Sure, no problem. Sing about a dumb girl getting creamed by a train? Let's do it. Royalties? Nah, you keep 'em . . ." The song made Mark Dinning a star for a Warholian quarter-hour while simultaneously destroying his budding career altogether.

The Song

"Teen Angel" may be the only love ballad that nobody can slow dance to. (Which may be a good thing because who'd want to?) It begins with Mark Dinning cooing "Teen angel, teen angel . . ." as a melancholy acoustic guitar strums each chord behind him. The music then drops into a quasi-Mexican vamp while Dinning sets up the situation at hand, that being a stalled car on the railroad tracks. The Teen Angel, all of sixteen and nameless, is pulled out of the car by her boyfriend as a speeding train races toward it; ". . . we were safe," Dinning warbles, "but you went running baaaack . . ."

Let's recap, shall we? Car stalls on railroad tracks, train approaches, couple gets out safely, girl runs back to car. There is a serious problem in narrative logic here because unless she left a nuclear warhead behind, there is no logical reason why anybody would do such a thing (keep this in mind, as I have a theory about it coming up). This clearly wasn't a wise decision. "Teen angel, can you see me?" Dinning sings longingly during the chorus, "Are you somewhere up above?" So it's official: The Teen Angel got smashed by the train only forty seconds into the song.

"What was it you were looking for?" Dinning inquires, asking the question on everybody's mind. A coroner, someone who normally doesn't make an appearance in any pop song, reveals the answer (though see also "DOA" by Bloodrock). He finds something in the Teen Angel's tiny fist that is returned to the bereaved boyfriend with great solemnity: the boy's high-school ring, which was "clutched" tightly in her fingers.

So there it is. The girl willingly stepped into the path of an oncoming White Freightliner to retrieve the high-school ring he gave to her. That's his story and he's sticking to it. Dinning mournfully tells us how he'll never be able to kiss her lips again, those same lips that uttered her last words to him: "Oh damn, I forgot something. I'll be right back." The song ends as quietly and irredeemably as it began. Two weeks after the recording of "Teen Angel," Mark Dinning had a number-one hit record and was singing it on *American Bandstand* in front of screaming teenagers. Two months after that, he was collecting unemployment.

Why It's Depressing

Since the American music industry was in a bad way during the early 1960s, it may explain the cultural naïveté that compelled record buyers to make this depressing song number one for fourteen weeks. Though it's better performed than "Tell Laura I Love Her," "Teen Angel" is saddled with the most egregious plot of the TCC songs. It's difficult to get past the implausibility that any girl would jump in front of a speeding train to retrieve a class ring. As high-school rings haven't changed much since the Louisiana Purchase, this means the Teen Angel sacrificed herself to retrieve one of those thick-banded sterling silver monstrosities you can use to punch open a safe. There's only one logical explanation: The Teen Angel was murdered.

That's right, I'm declaring this a clear-cut case of homicide right here and now. If Mark Dinning thinks I'm buying his claim that she ran back to the car on her own, he's dreaming. My theory is this: After months of malt shops and clammy hand-holding, the guy grows tired of his Teen Angel if only because she insists on being addressed as "Teen Angel." After telling her he wants to break up, she threatens to tell the school he's a Communist, a very big deal in 1960. Frustrated, the boy hatches a devilish plot and takes her for a car ride under the guise of reconciliation. He then knocks her out, parks in the middle of a railroad track, puts his class ring in her hand and gets out of the car just as the train is approaching. Crash! No more Teen Angel. Scoff you may, but this scenario makes far more sense than the preposterous tragedy Mark Dinning sings about. This is what makes "Teen Angel" so depressing, because justice has not been served. The little SOB got away with murder.

Last Kiss

Performed by J. Frank Wilson and the Cavaliers
Released 1964 (No. 1 in the US)
Performed by Pearl Jam
Released 1999 (No. 2 in the US)
Words and Music by Wayne Cochran

THE LAST OF the three Teenage Car Crash songs, the near-brilliant "Last Kiss" is hands-down the best and most tragic of the lot, and remains my personal favorite. Unlike its predecessors, there is no egregious lack of intelligence about the young couple whose lives are changed one fateful night. The song was superbly remade by Pearl Jam in 1998 and it was refreshing to hear Eddie Vedder sing a song while not sounding like a Teamster with a mouthful of novocaine. The real tragedy of "Last Kiss" lies with the artist who recorded the seminal hit version.

"Last Kiss" was written by the semi-legendary rockabilly artist Wayne Cochran, known for his flashy clothes and helmet-like platinum-colored hair. He'd read a newspaper article about a teenage girl who'd died in a car accident while out on a date and penned "Last Kiss" so that he could record it himself. Though he had a reputation for playing wild rockabilly, his 1964 version of "Last Kiss" was curiously bland and charted only modestly in regional markets. Then, a Texas-based rock group called J. Frank Wilson and the Cavaliers got ahold of the song and recorded a cover, and it was their version that became the national hit, going to number one in a matter of weeks. It was far superior to Cochran's tepid original because of its low-fidelity rawness (it was recorded in just five hours) and an unmistakable quality about lead singer J. Frank Wilson's voice: He sounded a little "off."

The Song

"Last Kiss" begins with its famous chorus of "Oh where oh where can my baby be . . . ?" over a thumping, clangy accompaniment supplied by the Cavaliers. Vocalist Wilson throws himself into the drama of the song, telling us how "the Lord took her away from me." Right away we know someone has perished, making this the only TCC song that gives away the ending at the beginning. Oddly enough, this actually works to the song's benefit, lending a "What happened?" urgency to its narrative.

The song begins innocently enough, with a young man and his girl driving together: "We were out on a date in my Daddy's car," Wilson sings in his edgy voice. Suddenly, the boy spies a stalled car in the middle of the road and tries to swerve around it, only to hear "the crying tires, the busting glass, the painful scream . . ." This is startling stuff and J. Frank Wilson's frantic voice gives it a disturbing sheen. He repeats the chorus, then flashes back to the aftermath once again. Wilson describes pouring rain and the blood running through his eyes as he gropes around trying to locate his girl. He finds her dying and lifts her head to where he can hear her. "Hold me, darling, just a little while," she whimpers to him. They share their last kiss before she dies in his arms. The chorus returns one final time, repeating its sad lament before fading out.

Why It's Depressing

Yowzah. How do you top a song like this? Well, you can't and nobody ever tried after "Last Kiss" except for maybe Bloodrock with the gruesome "DOA." Wilson's oddly bent vocals add just the right amount of pathos to the song, while the upbeat music doesn't compromise its tragic story. "Last Kiss" is easily the most successful of the TCC songs, and the Cavaliers' original holds up well alongside Pearl Jam's grungier remake. Everything about it works and you'll find yourself pleasantly depressed while listening to it. The inferior predecessors "Tell Laura I Love Her" and "Teen Angel" come off as immature melodramas and work today only as kitsch. "Last Kiss" has a timeless quality that even grumpy Pearl Jam was able to capture.

Wayne Cochran, the writer of "Last Kiss," continued performing in roadhouses and fairs before falling on hard times due to drinking and divorce. In 1981, he was able to turn his life around and left the rock stage for the pulpit, becoming a Christian minister. Alas, "Last Kiss" singer J. Frank Wilson did not fare as well. Even though the song was a number-one hit, both Wilson and the rest of the Cavaliers were stiffed in royalties. Their manager sued the record company, resulting in a paltry flat payout of only $3,000 (the lawyers earned vastly more). Like most of his contemporaries, Wilson was never able to chart another song and was consigned to one-hit-wonder status. By 1974, ten years after having the number-one single in the States, J. Frank Wilson was living in Lufkin, Texas, working as an orderly in a nursing home for $250 a week. "They took a little country boy," he was quoted as saying, "and put him in a big city with big money and he didn't know how to act. I had a hard life, but I learned, I learned."

Wilson died from alcoholism complications in 1991.

I Hate
Myself and
Want to Die

Good-bye to Love

Performed by the Carpenters
Released 1972 (No. 9 in the UK, no. 7 in the US)
Written by Richard Carpenter and John Bettis

THE CARPENTERS were the epitome of AM Lite during the 1970s, with music so creepily soothing that it pre-dated Prozac by seventeen years. The brother/sister musical duo sold 30 million records during their heyday, 29.9 million to parents who gave them to their teenage kids so they'd stop playing Alice Cooper. Once crucified by critics, the Carpenters have in recent years garnered more respect due to a collective realization about Karen Carpenter that was previously missed: Hands down, she has the most tragic voice in pop music history.

I'm being serious. Ms. Carpenter's melancholy sine wave vocals put meltdown divas like Mariah and Whitney to shame. Instead of over-the-top beltings, Karen sang every Carpenters song with sadness, resignation, and vibrato-free purity, as if she instinctively knew she was recording drivel and there wasn't a damn thing she could do about it. Her premature death at age thirty-two from anorexia robbed the music world of a genuine talent and Branson, Missouri, of a future headlining act. While the Carpenters produced enough cheery saccharine to float a yacht, Karen regularly injected an element of despondency into even their sunniest songs, and when she wrapped her heartrending voice around the misery-primed "Good-bye to Love," the results were almost incandescent.

The Song

"Good-bye to Love" was supposedly inspired by the movie musical *Rhythm on the . River*, featuring Bing Crosby as a songwriter whose most famous tune is entitled "Good-bye to Love." Curiously, the song is never heard in the movie, so Richard Carpenter and lyricist John Bettis borrowed the title to write their own composition.

They waste no time getting into full pity mode as the first notes you hear come from an oboe, still the worst instrument ever to infect popular music. It's fine for classical ensembles, but when you stick an oboe on a pop record, it's White Doves in Flight time except, in this case, all the doves are heading toward the spinning propeller on a Cessna. Karen's crystalline voice appears and promptly announces that nobody's ever cared if she lives or dies. Yikes. Even Kurt Cobain didn't get that fatalistic so quickly, and you immediately wonder what the hell's the problem. It seems Karen feels that love has passed her by all her life and the only thing she's ever known is how to live without it. These kind of heart-on-the-sleeve lyrics are very old-school Otis Redding, but the subtext of her performance takes the song to a whole new level where the message becomes clear: Karen Carpenter wants us all to jump off a bridge with her.

Richard Carpenter lords over the song like a muzak-obsessed Phil Spector, guiding his little sister through its busy melody over a bed of strings, harp glissandos, and cooing choirs, all the while oblivious that her jaw-dropping declarations like "all the years of useless search have finally reached an end" are weirding us out. Yes, he cowrote the song, yes, he knows it's sad, yes, he stuck a goddamned oboe on it without even blinking, yet Richard Carpenter is completely clueless to the fact that having Karen put her heartbreaking voice to it is like letting Courtney Love work nights at a pharmacy. Even the song's lone glimmer of hope, that the passing of time will allow her to find someone she can live for, rings hollow. Not for an instance do you think she believes that. No, Karen Carpenter is far more intent on jumping into the swirling waters below.

Things take a frightening turn with the sudden arrival of a bizarre guitar solo that threatens to push lovely Karen and the rest of us off the edge. A talented musician/arranger he may be, but I doubt Richard Carpenter would know a power chord from a power drill, and his decision to add a "rock" guitar solo to "Good-bye to Love" is so wrong it borders on the perverse. The guitarist, a studio hack with a fuzz pedal built by Mattel, ploddingly plays the song's melody for ten bars before suddenly going batshit and trying to channel Jeff Beck. Right when he's about to shove all of us into the river, his guitar is abruptly pulled out of the mix by a panicking engineer diving for the fader switch.

Karen wraps it all up with some dime-store philosophizing about how life is a "wheel of fortune" and how the future is "a mystery," blah, blah. She tries to reassure herself and us that one day she may feel differently but "for now this is my song." And, for now, she's climbed down off the bridge railing to head home to warm fondue and an episode of *All in the Family*, fully aware that the critics think she's not nearly as cool as Grace Slick.

Why It's Depressing

"Good-bye to Love" is less a song than a suicide note with a musical score. No other singer, be it Connie Francis or that scary chick from Evanescence, could've taken such mournful verses and transformed them into a Last Will and Testament. Karen Carpenter's voice is mixed so far up front, it makes your eardrums weep. Since she never employed any flashy vocal techniques, her singing is clear and soul-wrenching, like an ice sculpture melting under the lights. You can practically see her wandering through the glade in a long white dress as desiccated doves rain down around her, an oboe player with a bad complexion following her like a sheepdog. She eyes the distant bridge and wonders whether she should do a swan dive or a half gainer.

There was always something slightly unsettling about the Carpenters, beginning with their album covers, where the two of them beamed eerily at the camera like they were auditioning for *The Stepford Wives*. In hindsight, we now know what it was: Richard was happy, Karen was not. Despite being beautiful, talented (she was also a great drummer), and a millionaire at twenty-three, Karen Carpenter was a very sad girl whose only outlet was in the downbeat musings of "Good-bye to Love." It is no surprise that Richard Carpenter says it was her favorite song.

At Seventeen

Written and performed by Janis Ian
Released 1975 (No. 3 in the US)

SOMETIMES referred to as the original Jewel (gee, thanks), singer/songwriter Janis Ian was only fifteen years old when she scored a hit record in 1967 with her depressing interracial love song "Society's Child." Not wishing to rest on her teenage laurels, she outdid herself in a big way, breaking number three in 1975 with "At Seventeen," a self-loathing lounge song that tempted a whole generation of teenage girls to shove their heads into trash compactors. "At Seventeen" relates how, at age seventeen, Ms. Ian made the startling discovery that physically attractive people are more popular than unattractive people. (At eighteen, she found out that gravity makes things fall.) It remains one of the few, if not only, anthems for gawky adolescent girls who spend evenings alone gazing at the phone hoping some boy will call them (unless it's that sclerotic guy Chris from Algebra, in which case don't bother). It's also the only depressing song of note based on a samba beat, an incongruous musical choice akin to performing Megadeth in waltz time.

The Song

"At Seventeen" begins with an acoustic guitar vamping a bossa nova figure that's so Brazilian, you half expect her to break into "The Girl from Ipanema," to which this song bears an uncomfortable resemblance. Janis Ian sings, in a wispy soft voice that predates Norah Jones by nearly thirty years, about how "beauty queens" and "girls with ice cream smiles" are the only ones who ever find love, while describing herself as an acne-scarred twerp who never got a valentine and spent nights home alone pretending that guys were ringing her phone off the hook. But she's not bitter.

The lyrics begin to go off the rails when she introduces a brown-eyed girl wearing cast-off clothing who wanders in from God knows where to instruct Janis to "pity, please, the ones who serve. They only get what they deserve." While Ms. Ian feels sorry for herself, the brown-eyed girl pities wealthy trust-fund girls who get elected homecoming queen and end up marrying well and living comfortably. (Paging Van Morrison: Come and get your brown-eyed girl out of this song.) Soon, "At Seventeen" veers dangerously into Ramada Inn territory with a trumpet–trombone music break that sounds like two brass men who got lost on their way to a Burt Bacharach session. (They play their parts so tenuously, you can hear how embarrassed they are.) Nylon-string guitar filigrees push the lounge factor up several notches.

By the fourth stanza, Ms. Ian is channeling subgrade Stephen Sondheim rhymes: how snooty girls eventually lose out because of their "debentures of quality" and one can see their stunned expressions when "payment due exceeds accounts received." A free bottle of Zoloft to anyone who can explain what that means. She laments how she never got picked to play basketball and that, long ago, the world was younger than it is today. (Not to be picky, but wasn't everything?) At the song's end, she is left alone in her room, cheating at solitaire while still imagining that prospective lovers are calling her up to whisper dirty talk in her ear.

Why It's Depressing

"At Seventeen" is laden with 1970s singer/songwriter earnestness, the era of the canyon lady in a sundress who wouldn't take her Irish setter out for a walk until she put a bandanna around its neck. Clocking in at close to five minutes with no bridge, the song limps along in its quasi-Rio way, while milking its acoustic conceit so much you turn into a block of spruce just listening to it. The lyrics alternate between envying homecoming queens and condescending to them, as if Janis Ian can't make up her mind if she's feeling self-pity or defiance. Besides, I don't know of a single seventeen-year-old girl who would tell off the homecoming queen by saying she has debentures of quality; she'd call her a stuck-up bitch and key her Honda. Like most songs of the 1970s, "At Seventeen" became hoary three years into the Carter administration, back when rejected adolescents highlighted passages from *The Catcher in the Rye* instead of bringing a Beretta to school so they can shoot up the chemistry class.

Janis Ian is no slouch. By the time she really was seventeen, she was appearing on the *Tonight Show*, being written up in *Time* magazine and shopping for clothes with Janis Joplin, any of which, in my mind, beats the hell out of being a homecoming queen. Though a talented guitarist and prolific songwriter, she will always be identified with "At Seventeen" and still performs it to this day, to an audience whose own kids aren't even seventeen anymore.

One note: She released this bitter song in 1975 and, in a few short years, hot teenage girls like the kind she was jealous of were being carved into filets in all those *Halloween/Friday the 13th* slasher flicks.

I'm certain Janis Ian has a hockey mask buried in a closet at home.

My Immortal

Performed by Evanescence
Released 2003 (No. 7 in the UK and the US)
Written by Amy Lee, Ben Moody, and David Hodges

WHAT'S THE deal with contemporary piano ballads? When did they all start sounding like Pachelbel's Canon in D? Or maybe they always did, I'm not sure. Today, the sound of a lone Steinway at the beginning of a song is like those whooping sirens that let a submarine crew know they're about to get depth-charged. It's a sure sign you're going to be buried in a lot of heart-wrenching hooey courtesy of a tortured ingénue singing with her eyes shut so tightly you'd think she was welding without a mask. This scenario may not totally apply to Evanescence's "My Immortal" but it might as well. Any song that rhymes tears, fears, and years already has one foot in the pathos pit.

Evanescence was cofounded in Little Rock, Arkansas, in the late 1990s by singer/pianist Amy Lee and guitarist Ben Moody, the latter exiting the group suddenly in 2003. Fans describe the group's music as "epic dramatic goth pop/rock" or some such, because Lee has jet-black hair and dresses like she raided Stevie Nicks's closet. Her signature is a piercing soprano voice that would make a knock-knock joke sound like a Sylvia Plath poem. Evanescence hit the charts with their epic dramatic goth pop/rock single "Bring Me to Life," the perfect song to complement those annoying times when a teenage girl has to fend off an attack by Satan at four in the morning. The creepy strangeness of "Bring Me to Life" established Evanescence as a group that does nothing halfway and which does not have the word "sublime" in its vocabulary. So it was no surprise that the band's follow-up single was the depressing "My Immortal," a song that does for piano ballads what the *Hindenburg* did for zeppelin travel.

The Song

The first time I heard the self-pitying piano intro to "My Immortal," I could've bet my lungs that things weren't going to get any sunnier. Amy Lee is in mourning over the demise of her relationship with a former lover/companion/beau whatever, pleading "I wish that you would just leave," as "your presence still lingers here." She is all wounded and wracked with pain now, leading to the obligatory all-I-did-for-you mewlings that dumpees throw at dumpers to let the latter know how ungrateful they are. "When you cried," she sings during the chorus, "I'd wipe away all of your tears. When you screamed, I'd fight away all of your fears . . ." Aside from the lyrical felony of rhyming "tears" with "fears" (the second worst cliché behind "heart" and "torn apart"), this disturbing stanza indicates that the guy she's pining for must be a total whack job. If you spent half your together time with someone either getting him to stop crying or watching him tear his hair out in reaction to whatever phobia he's afflicted with ("Ohmigod! I'm wearing synthetics!!"), wouldn't you seriously think that maybe you could do better? "My Immortal" becomes an ode to codependency, with Amy Lee relishing how she passed up ten normal guys just to be with a complete loon she found "fascinating."

They had memorable times together throughout their torrid relationship. We know this by how much Amy felt captivated by "your resonating light," making it the only time in the history of physics that light waves have ever resonated. But now the light has stopped, er, resonating (however that works) and she's left with her dreams haunted by "your face" and her sanity crumbling from the memory of "your voice." "My Immortal" never goes anywhere musically, with Ms. Lee instead putting all her energies into making her wounded Inner Child wail like a foghorn. You can practically see her writhing on the studio floor in full epic dramatic goth pop/rock glory, while Ben Moody nudges his chorus pedal out of the way so she doesn't actually swallow it. In short, Amy Lee is totally losing her young gothic mind and seems awfully damn proud of it. This may explain why she feels inclined to dwell on all the times she held his hand through the years, dabbed his tears, chased his fears, oiled his gears, boxed his ears, sharpened his shears, ignored his sneers, and bought all his beers because he never had any money.

Why It's Depressing

"My Immortal" is a prime example of a relationship song that follows what I call the Quantum Tragedy Paradigm: The shorter the relationship between two people, the more overwrought and tragic the song that describes it. Judging by the tanker load of anguish that Amy Lee spews in "My Immortal," I estimate she broke up with someone she went out with for about an hour, a guy who, if her lyrics are even remotely accurate, was one big loser.

If we utilize the Quantum Tragedy Paradigm, we can approximate the arc of Ms. Lee's relationship with her nameless infatuation.

8 P.M.: Amy Lee meets a sullen, pale tattoo victim named _____ at Club Dirge in West Hollywood, dressed head to toe in black with a piercing through his clavicle ("they used a drill . . .").

8:07 P.M.: Amy and _____ consummate relationship in a wraparound booth. She tells *People* magazine _____ is her soul mate. He tells friends he's banging the chick who sings in "that band Effervescent."

8:19 P.M.: Amy and _____ move in together. She takes _____ on the road with Evanescence. _____ cries and throws tantrums during concerts because Amy won't talk to him while she's onstage. Other group members start calling him Yoko.

8:28 P.M.: Amy takes _____ on extended vacation at end of tour. Discovers he suffers from epiphasphincterphobia: the fear of other people figuring out you're an asshole. Trip cut short as they're unable to find hotel where staff won't laugh at him.

8:37 P.M.: Amy catches _____ *in flagrante* with lesser-known Hilton sister Kiki and throws him out of house. Lets him back in after he stands on lawn threatening to kill himself. Neighbors sue her for preventing him from making good on his threat.

8:48 P.M.: _____ accuses Amy of not being supportive when she declines to record song he wrote for her group. She tells him she cannot, with a clear conscience, sing anything entitled "Wax My Pole, Bitch." _____ goes into hysterics and has hallucinations about being a mediocrity. Amy tells him he's a genius, if only to coax him out of the linen closet.

8:55 P.M.: _____ forges Amy's signature and puts down payment on BMW. He totals it backing out of dealership lot. She reminds him that he's still a genius.

9 P.M.: Amy comes home to find _____ has moved out, leaving his "presence" and three subpoenas behind. Distraught, she sits down at piano and writes "My Immortal." Song becomes a hit and she stars in music video shot in (natch) black and white. Evanescence cofounder Ben Moody quits group shortly thereafter.

It Must Be Him

Performed by Vicki Carr
Released 1967 (No. 2 in the UK, no. 3 in the US)
Music by Gilbert Bécaud
French lyrics by Maurice Vidalin
English lyrics by Mack David

AS THE ONLY song that can cause a feminist to kill herself, then roll over in her grave, "It Must Be Him" is the ultimate anthem for doormats everywhere and has my vote for the most pathetic tune ever written. While there are many overblown songs about unrequited love, this depressing pop meltdown reigns over them all like Bismarck. "It Must Be Him" was a huge hit single for singer Vicki Carr that appealed to a zeitgeist I had no idea ever existed. Were there really that many people willing to buy a record about the anxieties of a desperate, clingy woman? Evidently so, as the song charted at number three in America and England, and received four Grammy nominations. (Singer Shirley Bassey also released a version of "It Must Be Him" the same year, which landed in the Top 40.) As the flip side to the Lillith Fair, "It Must Be Him" is all about a woman whose entire life revolves around the men in her life and who is willing to lay her dignity aside just to put them on a pedestal.

Vicki Carr was born in El Paso, Texas, to a Mexican-American family and scored her first hit in the early 1960s with "He's A Rebel." But it wasn't until she forsook all her dignity to record the appalling "It Must Be Him" that she found mainstream success. It was originally a French song entitled "Seul sur son Etoile," which singer Gilbert Bécaud recorded in

1966. (I've never bothered listening to it because there's no way it could be more degrading than Ms. Carr's version.) While normally it takes years for something to become kitsch, "It Must Be Him" earned the label on the day of its release and the passage of time has only made the song worse (or better, depending on how sick you are).

The Song

"It Must Be Him" was released in 1967, which remains a watershed year in American music. I'm not talking about the Summer of Love (good guess, though). I'm referring to how 1967 was the year that featured the worst studio engineering in pop music history. Listen to any Grateful Dead, Blue Cheer, or Big Brother and the Holding Company album of the time and you'll hear just how widespread LSD was back then; even the engineers were tripping. To be honest, most rock music albums from the 1960s were blown away by their non-rock counterparts, be it Tony Bennett, Nina Simone, or the Golden Gate Quartet, in terms of studio production, and this is certainly the case with "It Must Be Him." The song boasts beautifully rich string textures and crisp percussion, expertly blended with Vicki Carr's soaring voice. Such attention to detail, however, makes its lyrical humiliation that much more perverse because it's so well executed.

"It Must Be Him" begins with Carr trying to convince herself that she must move on from Mr. Wrong: "I tell myself, 'what's done is done,' " she sings determinedly, declaring that she'll play the field from now on and "play it cool," too. I'm no chump, she tells herself, noting how it's better if "he" stays away. She's a part of the 1960s sexual revolution, a post–*Sex and the Single Girl* chick with capris, go-go boots, and Twiggy hair. Naturally, she's kidding herself because when the phone rings, her mantra of empowerment dissolves. Her martini glass crashing to the floor, she races across the room to the receiver, grazing her adorable shin on a coffee table along the way. Grabbing the phone, she prays, "Let it please be him. Dear God, it must be him, it must be him or I shall die!" It's not him.

It's apparent that this woman is in denial but being that it's 1967 and "in denial" hasn't entered the public lexicon yet, we'll settle for "she doesn't grok* herself." And who among us hasn't failed to grok how to deal with the passive-aggressive dipshits in our lives? She cannot live without her guy, a ruthless self-involved jerk who toys with her fragile emotions.

They probably first met at a Jasper Johns retrospective in a SoHo art gallery. She found that he shared her passion for novelist Thomas Pynchon, both having read *The Crying of Lot 49* through page 73 before giving up like I did. Naturally, the bastard's married, but this doesn't stop her from having an affair with him. Three months later, she's alone in her TriBeCa apartment, clad in tear-stained chemise, playing Astrid Gilberto albums over and over while waiting for the phone to ring. Every time it does, it's not him.

The woman regains her composure and tries for self-affirmation one more time, gazing into the mirror while saying, "he'll never hurt me anymore. I'm not a puppet on a string . . ." There are plenty of guys who'd love to be with a classy woman like her—*rrrinnnng*.

The chorus returns as she breaks the sound barrier rushing to the phone. "Let it please be him. Dear God . . ." she cries aloud. It's not. "And then I die, again I die." The orchestra thunders behind Ms. Carr as she collapses into a heap on the shag carpeting.

---

* From Robert Heinlein's *Stranger in a Strange Land*.

Why It's Depressing

In order to understand "It Must Be Him," try to imagine yourself as a fragile, needy woman whose entire life revolves around the sparse attentions of a selfish guy who . . .

On second thought, don't try to understand "It Must Be Him" because it really isn't worth it. There's no logical reason in the world why anyone would write a song like this except to hope it becomes a featured number in an all-male drag revue. It's one of those depressing tunes in which there are only two ways to perform it—totally sincere or over-the-top campy—both are deadly. There are no gray areas or ambiguous emotions in "It Must Be Him," with no turning of the tables or O. Henry surprise ending. The song simply showcases the servility of a young woman smitten with a guy who mispronounces her name and forgets her birthday. Plus, the utter desperation Vicki Carr employs in her voice makes for a disturbing listening experience.

In many ways, she sounds a lot like Alex Forrest, the spurned woman from the 1985 film *Fatal Attraction*, except that she lacks the ambition to boil a child's rabbit or leap out of a bathtub with a knife in her hand. All she can do is sob and stare at the phone.

Today, "It Must Be Him" is bascially all but forgotten, yet it still has the power to stun and debilitate. Women, don't even try to go near it. Forget feeling depressed, you'll break your hands punching them through the wall.

One

Performed by Metallica
Released 1989 (No. 13 in the UK, no. 35 in the US)
Words and music by James Hetfield and Lars Ulrich

FOR SUCH an atavistic musical form, heavy metal has spawned a lot of subgenres, including speed metal, death metal, glam metal, hardcore, black metal, thrash metal, and ambient metal, a kind of head-banging music for John Tesh fans. Not surprisingly, metal bands have never featured a lot of mirth in their music (though I must give props to the group that made an attempt with its song "Fun with a Dead Nun"). Even their fans tend to be hyper-serious:

> "Metal as a pattern of thought is a rebellion within post-modern ideology from structured cyclicism to structuralist dynamicism, effectively extending the principles of modernism to a post-relativity universe through a focus on transcendental kineticism, individual participation in post-moral experience, and chaotic mass destruction."[*]

Interesting, but I think the following from the same essay sums up metal philosophy more succinctly:

> "When drinking blood, be sure to have it chilled, or else it will curdle."

---

[*] From www.anus.com

This brings us to Metallica, arguably the most successful heavy metal act in music history, who survived the post-'80s metal malaise because they didn't suck like many of their glam-cursed colleagues. The group had already garnered respectable album sales and a substantial following when they released their 1988 album . . . *And Justice for All*, which went multi-platinum. In an effort to get airplay though, some chucklehead released their nightmarish song "One" as a single, prompting Metallica to produce their first music video. This is significant because viewing the video for "One" amps up your depression considerably (more on that in a bit).

Metallica raised the morbidness bar dramatically when they composed "One," as the song is based on the world's most depressing book, *Johnny Got His Gun*. You'll not find any work that'll ruin your reading hours more than Dalton Trumbo's 1939 novel; it makes Foxe's *Book of Martyrs* read like Candace Bushnell. I was assigned this didactic anti-war screed in high-school English and, upon finishing it, concluded that the only thing more depressing than being an armless, legless war veteran with no face who's blind, deaf, and mute, is being forced to read about one. Parents' groups have accused heavy metal bands of promoting devil worship in their music for years but, personally, I think Metallica would've been better off borrowing from some demonic book on goat slaughtering than Trumbo's novel. Lucifer offers a lot more laughs.

The Song

Johnny Got His Gun is narrated in the first person by a soldier named Joe Bonham who's in an army hospital after being horribly wounded by a shell that exploded in a trench. He's lost his face, all of his limbs, and every one of his five senses. Joe is fed through a tube and basically ignored until a nurse notices him tapping Morse code with his head. He makes numerous requests, including that they kill him, but all are denied. (You now know the entire book but feel free to read it if you're a sucker for this kind of stuff.) Metallica more or less follows the book's concept in "One," opening the song with the sounds of machine-gun fire and helicopters, the latter an unknown commodity during World War I, where Trumbo's novel is set. The combat noises sound suspiciously Nintendo-like, but that doesn't offset the skull-crushing gloom that soon follows.

The introduction to "One" runs close to two minutes, tricking you several times before any singing is heard. Somber minor-key guitar patterns are played over, while lead player Kirk Hammett inserts nervous pithy fills (using the sad Dorian mode, the cheeky fiend). This goes on for several bars until the band throws in its first musical trick, modulating to the relative major and adding salubrious nylon-string guitars. For a brief moment, "One" sounds halfway reflective until the group suddenly remembers its Ozzy heritage and returns to the grim dealings at hand: the interior monologue of a mutilated faceless man.

James Hetfield, with his terminal grimace of a voice, sings of not remembering anything or knowing whether he's dreaming or "if this is true . . ." Of course it's true, and he tries to show his displeasure by screaming, but is stopped by a "terrible silence." Like Joe Bonham, the narrator of "One" informs us that he, too, was in a war and there's not much left of him now except chronic pain. He cannot see, cannot hear, cannot wander into Guitar Center on Sunset Boulevard and pull a Strat off the wall so he can bash out this song like so many metalheads did in 1990 when "One" was everywhere. The chorus, what there is of it, has the narrator wishing for death while asking God to wake him from his nightmare. (The major key section from the intro always reappears at the end of the chorus, toying with us further.) Each new stanza borrows images from the Trumbo book, including "tubes that stick in me" and references to being a "novelty" of wartime, a major plot point in the novel. "Please God, help me . . ." he screams, the same pitiful mantra Joe Bonham runs repeatedly inside his head. (To call "One" the world's first heavy metal set of Cliff Notes wouldn't be inaccurate.)

The music builds in intensity and Metallia begins what they do better than any band: rip off your head. Double-tracked guitars, run-through distortion pedals designed by Northrup, stomp through the song's twisted melody while drummer Lars Ulrich bashes his trap set like he just found out about Napster. They eventually blast into an entirely different percussive section where Hetfield basically loses it. "Darkness! Imprisoning me!" he roars. "Absolute horror!" The band pummels along with each syllable while we hear the extent of the narrator's injuries. A landmine (less wordy than "errant shell fired into trench") was responsible for blowing off all his limbs while depriving him of his "sight," "speech," and "hearing." Now his soul is gone and he's left with a "life in hell . . ." At this point, Metallica gets weary of Trumbo's book and tears into a mind-boggling speed metal jam that rewrites Einstein's laws of space/time continuum. The playing is so bone-crunching, you could implode a building with it, and Hammett's soloing is particularly scary. The onslaught builds with stop/start panic until banging to an abrupt conclusion. "One" doesn't end so much as stop—the way a Corvette stops when it runs into a semi.

Why It's Depressing

Borrowing anything from *Johnny Got His Gun* makes for a depressing time and the fact that "One" utilizes the novel's most grim aspects is what separates it from Metallica's usual downbeat fare. Adding to the portent is Hetfield's snarling vocals. Like so many metal frontmen, he incorporates a strained singing style that sounds like he's dead-lifting a Clydesdale. He's difficult to understand at times, too, squaring his vowels to the point that "me" becomes "may," "real" becomes "rail," and so on (. . . *And*

Justice for All has such a sterile mix to it, you'd think the engineer was a germaphobe who sprayed bleach on the soundboard before he touched a knob). Still, it's to the band's credit that their playing is so chillingly expert (you can never deny them their musicianship) and you'll throw your neck out trying to bob along with it.

The real baptism by fire for depressed listeners of "One" is to watch the video. Not content with borrowing from Trumbo's book, they also used scenes from the 1971 film *Johnny Got His Gun*, which the author wrote and directed. While the band lip-syncs inside a dark warehouse—the kind normally found in serial killer movies—clips from the film are interspersed throughout, mostly featuring the masked torso of Timothy Bottoms trying to method-act his way out of a hospital bed. He screams, he cries, he panics, he thrashes, he has dream sequences, he wishes he could start work on *The Last Picture Show*. Metallica lifts every scenery-chewing moment out of the film and drops it into their rib-rattling song. A dispiriting flop, the movie disappeared quickly, but a whole new generation of headbangers were reintroduced to it and I've no doubt video rentals of *Johnny Got His Gun* were brisk for a while. But the rest of us mortals who stumbled across "One" while channel surfing witnessed the monochromatic miseries of a dismembered man while wondering how Hetfield could sing with his teeth clenched like that. Plus, I was reminded again of that book, that book . . .

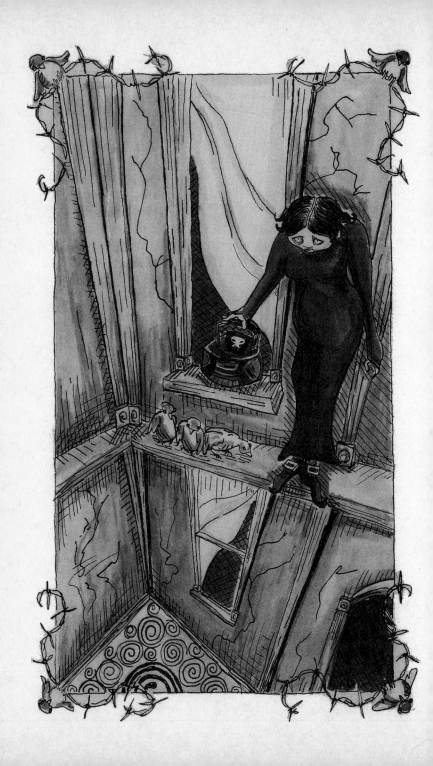

I'm trying to Be
Profound
and touching, But

Really Suck

at It

Round Here

Performed by Counting Crows
Released 1994 (No. 10 in the US)
Written by Adam Duritz, David Byron, Dave Janusko,
Dan Jewett, and Chris Roldan

"ROUND HERE" established the Berkeley-based Counting Crows as one of the music industry's biggest acts, while simultaneously establishing Adam Duritz as its sulkiest lead singer. The early 1990s was the brief era of grunge and alternative rock, which eventually faded after the public grew bored with the I-despise-success posings doled out by Duritz, Eddie Vedder, Kurt Cobain, Layne Staley, Chris Cornell, Zack De La Rocha, et al, scowling frontmen who attended music award shows for the sake of appearing annoyed about being there. Of this lot, Adam Duritz is unquestionably the most neurotic. His band's debut album was the biggest-selling CD of 1994, he had the cast of *Friends* appearing in the band's videos, he dated Jennifer Aniston. So what does he do? Screws up his hair.

"Round Here" is prototypical Duritz, containing all the elements that established him as the Holden Caulfield of the slacker set, while sounding like it was written according to an alt-rock song checklist: Despairing yet obscure lyrics? Check. Jangly guitar figure? Check. Passing suicide reference? Check. Ennui? Check. Duritz strip-mined this territory longer than most of his contemporaries because, unlike them, his band didn't break up and he never killed himself. But when he started coming across like Dustin Hoffman in *Rain Man* during concerts, critics, confidants, and close friends finally suggested that he LIGHTEN UP. To a certain degree he has, but his hair is still a disaster.

The Song

I'm breaking format with "Round Here" by not going through it in order from beginning to end. It doesn't matter. Sure, everyone likes the haunting guitar lick that carries it along but nobody really knows what this song's about anyway, other than there's a crazy girl named Maria who's hanging out with Duritz. She spends her days taking off her clothes outside houses while declaring "she's close to understanding Jesus." She cries a lot, threatens to throw herself off buildings, has "trouble acting normal when she's nervous," etc. So, yeah, Maria's a little odd. She's not very bright, either, since Duritz sings how she left Nashville and came all the way to the West Coast to find a guy "who looks like Elvis" (correct me if I'm wrong, but isn't Memphis right down the highway from Nashville?).

I'm pretty certain that Maria ended up in Los Angeles since the insane love to come here. She likely settled in Venice where "the ocean meets the land" and the homeless have a home. During the song's chorus, we hear about all the great things people can do "round here." They can stand up straight, radiate, stay up late, never wait, carve names, look the same—Duritz has a weakness for this rhyme scheme. There's also a mention of being sacrificed like lambs, which means that Counting Crows has probably met the president of their record company.

Though it's clear Maria needs a suite at the Hotel Lithium, it doesn't help her situation that she's hanging around Adam Duritz, the Isaac Newton of delirium. While she sits in the corner sketching the Rapture with a crayon, Duritz is getting us lost in the song's opening verse where someone steps out into the fog like a ghost: "No one notices the contrast of white on white," he sings mournfully, not realizing he doesn't know the definition of the word "contrast." He describes walking through air, between the rain, through himself, then says

"Where? I don't know?" Meanwhile, Maria gets upset when she notices she's out of burnt sienna.

The music briefly kicks itself out of its misery during the funky bridge, yet Duritz stays firmly on the gloom path, suggesting that all little children should "run like hell," if only to get away from his hair. The song winds up (or down, in this case) with Maria having a complete break from reality. She's hearing voices now and stands in a parking lot asking passersby to shoot her. "Can't you see my walls are crumbling?" she says. Yes dear, we can, and the sooner you get the hell out of LA, the better you'll feel.

Why It's Depressing

Los Angeles has plenty of disturbed women like Maria. Half of them are homeless, the rest executive assistants at television networks. For Adam Duritz to narrate their personal stories is like having him lead a museum tour: You just know he's going to steer his group away from the exhibits so he can take them into the basement to gaze at the furnace. Of course, this only applies if that's what "Round Here" is about because I'm still not sure. I'm not sure of anything after Duritz tells us how "the angels get a better view of the crumbling difference between wrong and right." How is it that secular new age pantheists are the only ones who know where the angels are and what they're doing? When he starts caterwauling that someone needs to catch him because he's falling, I'm wondering if perhaps he's more screwed up than the Maria in his song.

Maybe there is no Maria, never was. Perhaps she's simply Duritz's female alter ego, albeit one who sulks less and weeps more. Maybe the voices in her head are actually in his own head, all of them complaining that they should be getting SAG scale. The one thing I know for certain is that "Round Here" makes for a depressing experience every time it comes on the radio because Maria's screaming at spoons, Duritz is misinformed about the definition of "contrast," and the angels still have a better view of crumbling differences than I do. And I live "round here."

Lucky Man

Performed by Emerson Lake & Palmer
Released 1971 (No. 48 in the US)
Written by Greg Lake

A CAUTIONARY tale of royal hubris, the hoary song "Lucky Man" pops up regularly on FM stations devoted to "classic rock" (you know them by the DJs who are able to spin "Stairway to Heaven" four times a week without going postal). It tells the tragic story of a wealthy nobleman who discovers that all his material goods and possessions cannot save him from death in battle. Either that or it's about an obnoxious rich bastard who gets shot by his own troops. "Lucky Man" is the closing track on Emerson Lake & Palmer's 1971 debut album, a bombastic work featuring more organ solos than Easter mass at the Vatican. ELP epitomized the so-called "progressive" rock of the early 1970s, with its Bach-on-amphetamines concert jams, deafening sound systems, light shows, and Moog synthesizers the size of the Chrysler building.

The Song

As a 1970s prog rock song, "Lucky Man" is somewhat of an anomaly because you can actually make sense of the lyrics (I defy anyone to explain what Yes's "mountains come out of the sky and they stand there" means). Over a wistful twelve-string guitar lick, vocalist Greg Lake plaintively tells us about a gentleman of means endowed with stables filled with white horses, who spends his days having scores of satin-dressed ladies glide into his bedroom for some Edwardian-era group nookie. The chorus is simple: "Oooooooh, what a lucky man he was!" To drive home the point of just how lucky this guy was, Greg Lake overdubs his voice 13,958 times to create a virtual Lake-ernacle choir. We know he's lucky because his bed is stuffed with the finest goose down while sheets of the sheerest lace make up the "gold-covered mattress on which he was laid." Now, there is a lucky man.

We're meant to admire the Lucky Man, a pampered sybarite who screams at the servants and makes every young lass crawl under white lace prior to servicing him. Still, there's the problem with the lyric "on which he was laid." There are two interpretations of this line, one colloquial, one prepositional. The former reminds us what the Lucky Man has done to him daily on his gold-covered mattress; we figured that out when we heard about the ladies lined up outside his door. The latter hints that the Lucky Man was unable to get into bed on his own and had to be placed there. Was he reeling from an all-night Bordeaux bender or did one of his white horses toss him during a ride through the shire?

Alas, we never know, for there's a serious turn of events. It seems that the Lucky Man finds himself heading off to war, to fight for honor and glory at the Western Front. The townspeople, whose own daughters were made to fellate this high-maintenance twit, line the streets waving cheerfully while singing at the top of their lungs as he marches away: "OOOOOOOH, WHAT A LUCKY MAN HE WAS!"

Greg Lake implies the Lucky Man nobly volunteered to head into battle, but I suspect the hedonistic prick was dragged off to the trenches screaming in protest. Being wealthy and lazy, he's made an officer and dropped off at the Somme river with 150-odd lice-ridden infantrymen under his command. While haranguing a sergeant-major about rat droppings in his bangers and mash, his luck finally runs out when a bullet drops him like a deer. Who fells the Lucky Man is a mystery, either a German sniper or an annoyed Tommy who shot him so he'd stop bitching. Mortally wounded, he staggers about the trench crying for first aid while his men contemplate throwing him up out of the trench so the Huns can finish him off with a burst of mustard gas. The Lucky Man finally collapses and dies. Yep, there's one lucky man for you.

The song should otherwise end there except for the arrival of the most demented instrumental break ever to appear on a rock record, namely a Moog synthesizer cadenza that comes screaming in like Hell's theremin after the final chorus. Cranked loud enough, it will cause whales to beach themselves. After several bars of ear-splitting synth babble, the song basically falls apart and concludes with a sloppy drum crash. It is one of the weirdest endings to a song ever recorded.

Why It's Depressing

ELP are at their best when they go lunatic on classical themes, but Greg Lake's acoustic numbers can get turgid—think James Taylor channeled through Mussorgsky. Despite his prog-rock roots with King Crimson, Lake has always appeared to me as a frustrated folk-pop singer who would've been happier partnering up with Jim Croce and playing "Time in a Bottle." ELP's performance of "Lucky Man" lies somewhere between dirge and lumber, and Lake's vocal delivery is so earnest, he sounds like he's explaining to a five-year-old why the family dog had to be put to sleep. In addition, you have the challenge of making the listener mourn the death of a guy who probably cheated on his taxes and talked way too loudly in restaurants.

Then there's the aforementioned synthesizer solo which, after thirty-four years, still sounds like a defective smoke alarm. Whatever compelled keyboardist Keith Emerson, an otherwise virtuoso musician, to throw in this sawtooth atrocity, I'll never know. Was he overwrought by the Lucky Man's demise? Did Greg Lake break his harpsichord? Emerson has claimed in interviews that he ad-libbed the solo in one take.

I believe him.

Beth

Performed by KISS
Released 1976 (No. 7 in the US)
Written by Peter Criss, Stan Penridge, and Bob Ezrin

ONCE IN a while, scientists discover new things that force them to rewrite the textbooks. The discovery of the muon revealed that the electron wasn't the smallest sub-atomic particle after all. Likewise, the song "Beth" made audiences realize that KISS didn't just do hard rock songs that sucked hippo poop. They were also capable of doing poignant piano ballads that sucked hippo poop. The group gets extra nose-tweakings for conjuring up this depressing, sappy tune because it's about a young woman who feels lonely and abandoned because her boyfriend is . . . at band rehearsal.

The vast majority of KISS fans who swooned to "Beth" when it was first released did not understand this. They were too busy being agog that the era's nuttiest heavy metal act had recorded a ballad and even more stunned that Peter Criss, the band's drummer, was singing it. Everyone knew KISS was all about their campy stage shows, complete with sci-fi S&M outfits, homicidal clown makeup, and Gene Simmons's fire-eating/blood-puking shtick. Audiences went to KISS concerts for one reason only: so they could say they had.

The Song

"Beth" was written years before its 1976 release and is supposedly based on a musician in Peter Criss's earlier band, Chelsea, whose wife kept interrupting rehearsals with phone calls (the original lyrics were supposedly very negative but KISS producer Bob Ezrin rewrote the verses to make the song less hostile). Any woman married to a musician is in one of the worst social situations possible. Having known musicians all my life, I can say there are two kinds: those who don't work so they're pissed off, and those who do but not as musicians so they're still pissed off. "Beth" is about the former because Peter Criss has openly admitted that prior to KISS, he didn't work and practiced the drums while his then wife supported him. I find this surprising, if only because he said he actually practiced.

The song opens with a piano accompaniment (played by producer Ezrin) that never strays below middle C on the keyboard, giving it a tinkling quality that sounds like a music box set on stun. Soon strings, woodwind, and horns enter into the mix, an incongruous addition to any KISS song since it's like putting shellac on barf. "Beth, I hear you calling," Criss sings, before crawling out from behind the drum kit to get on the phone and tell her that he cannot come home just yet. The band is still rehearsing, he tells her, and darned if they "just can't find the sound." This is one of the more astonishing verses in "Beth" since anyone who's ever listened to KISS knows that finding the right "sound" was never a big priority to them. It'll only be a few more hours, he promises her, while the band yells at him to get off the phone. "Oh Beth, what can I do?" he laments before hanging up.

Beth has gone through this before. Many an evening she's waited at home alone while the jobless wonder is over in a basement somewhere banging away. "Didn't I put the down-payment on his Ludwig trap set?" she grumbles. "Didn't I buy him that new ride cymbal? This isn't fair." She phones again and Criss tries to be understanding. He admits that he's hardly ever with her but swears it'll just be a few more hours and then he'll be home. He hangs up and the band chastises him about his clingy wife. "Tell her to stop calling so much," they say. "We need time to figure out 'Strutter.' "

After an instrumental interlude (more shellac), the song ends with Beth finding out that it won't be just a few more hours. Instead, Peter and the boys are going to be playing all night, still searching for the elusive sound, whatever the hell it is. She hangs up heartbroken and goes to bed, while Ezrin's piano and string arrangement plinks its way to a conclusion.

Why It's Depressing

What makes "Beth" so dispiriting? For starters, Peter Criss sings it. I know he helped write the song but, please, the guy carries a tune the way a Vespa carries a truck transmission. Besides, I thought only the Beatles stuck their drummer with the worst songs (Ringo and "Octopus's Garden" anyone?). But the main issue is how so much time and energy went into a song about a relationship being compromised by band rehearsal. Having done time in several rock outfits over the years, I've met women like Beth before. She was usually married to the biggest complainer in the group, a dyspeptic guy who bitched about my Farfisa organ and thought we should do more Journey covers. The composite Beth usually worked as a nurse or secretary in an insurance office and got married to King A-hole right out of high school, hoping his mediocre musical abilities would amount to great things. In Peter Criss's case, great things did happen and he thanked his wife for her years of support by divorcing her at the height of KISS's success.

One of my most vivid memories from childhood was seeing KISS perform on a 1977 primetime TV variety special hosted by Paul Lynde, the flamboyant gay comedic actor most remembered for being the center square on *Hollywood Squares*. Watching Peter Criss in full feline glory lip-sync his way through "Beth" while pretending to play the piano was a depressing marvel, even better than the band's awkward mime job to "Detroit Rock City" (in KISS's defense, every rock band was forced to lip-sync on TV back then). The best part was seeing Gene, Paul, and Ace walk up to their comrade after he finished, patting his shoulders to comfort him for reliving Beth's torment while leaving the audience with the erroneous impression that Peter Criss was a sensitive soul and he knew how to play the piano.

Nowadays, no group would dare commit such an outright act of cheesiness but this was pre-irony, back when American television had only three networks. Most of the nation who tuned into the Paul Lynde variety special got to see KISS glumly deadpanning their way through a mock interview with a flustered Lynde while *The Brady Bunch*'s Florence Henderson twiddled her thumbs nearby. This is why 1970s nostalgia is still a dangerous thing.

MacArthur Park

Performed by Richard Harris
Released 1968 (No. 4 in the UK, no. 2 in the US)
Rereleased 1972 (No. 38 in the UK)
Performed by Donna Summer
Released 1978 (No. 5 in the UK, no. 1 in the US)
Words and Music by Jimmy Webb

I WANTED to begin this section on the infamous "MacArthur Park" with a smug joke about how nobody knows what the song is about, but I discovered I was thirty-five years too late. Today the joke has become a scientific fact: Nobody knows what "MacArthur Park" is about except that it has that spine-crawling refrain about a cake being left out in the rain. For that matter, people aren't even sure if it ever was a song or just an operetta that stumbled into the wrong room on singles night. It does have the ignoble distinction of being voted the worst song of all time in a 1997 poll of 10,000 readers conducted by humorist Dave Barry. That's a lot of bile, but I feel it's unfair and, besides, it lets Carole Bayer Sager off the hook. "MacArthur Park" isn't remotely the worst song, though it's certainly the most bombastic of depressing songs and I must give kudos to the man who conceived this musical melodrama when he was only twenty-one.

For a time, Jimmy Webb was the most famous songwriter in America, the enfant terrible of pop music. He wrote and produced Fifth Dimension's 1966 hit "Up, Up, and Away" when he was barely out of his teens. Webb went on to pen a slew of top-ten hits over the next few years, including the brilliant "Wichita Lineman," a number-one hit for Glen

Campbell and the first existential country tune. Influenced by Burt Bacharach, his songs bordered on architectural, filled with startling bridges, frequent modulations, and melodies that could make statues change positions. Musically gifted to the point of being scary, Webb's Achilles' heel was sometimes his lyrics, which varied from great ("Wichita Lineman") to exasperating (this song). Still, one must consider that Webb peaked very early in his career, writing his most famous songs before he was twenty-five, so his talent had not yet matured. Unfortunately, changing music trends caused his star to recede by the end of the 1970s, and nowadays his Byzantine composing style (i.e., using actual harmony and melody) is considered passé in this era of two-note trip hop. Yet Jimmy Webb's legacy as one of pop music's most idiosyncratic songwriters remains intact, with much of it resting on what is considered his magnum opus, "MacArthur Park."

Webb produced the song independently and hired his drinking buddy, Irish actor Richard Harris (King Arthur in *Camelot*), to sing it. He pitched the record to major record companies, where it was roundly rejected. At over seven minutes in length with lyrics straight out of the Institute of Warped Metaphors, "MacArthur Park" sounded like three separate songs stitched together by a stoned seamstress (and it still does, believe me). Everyone felt "MacArthur Park" had zero potential for Top 40 success until producer Lou Adler picked up the song for his Dunhill Records label and released it at its original seven-minute-plus length, unheard of at the time. The song went on to reach number two in the charts in 1968, astonishing everyone. (Donna Summer went to number one ten years later with her silly disco version.) Since then, "MacArthur Park" hasn't aged well and is ubiquitously loathed today for its excesses. The only way you're likely to ever hear it is if you go to Jimmy Webb's house and ask him to sing it for you.

The Song

"MacArthur Park" is difficult to analyze because, quite honestly, it's so damned weird. According to Webb, it's about a man lamenting the end of a relationship, which inspires a litany of if-you-say-so reactions from haters of the song. It begins with one of the most recognizable introductions ever, a solo piano playing minor chords against a descending bass line. Though he all but created it, Webb's intro has been so overused that people assume he stole it. "Spring was never waiting for us, girl," Richard Harris sings tremulously. "It ran one step ahead . . ." Spring, running—all of this is very 1960s groove-with-nature stuff filtered through Webb's trademark solipsism. Already, he bewilders us with the most awkward phrase to ever grace a pop song: ". . . we followed in the dance between the parted pages and were pressed . . ." The couple, it appears, is being pressed by "love's hot fevered iron like a striped pair of pants" (no, I did not type that wrong). As Harris continues, he recalls an organic hippie girl with long Joni Mitchell hair kneeling in the grass holding a tiny bird in her hand while old men are playing checkers (no, I did not type that wrong). Either Jimmy Webb was cribbing images off a Salvador Dali painting while he was writing this or Richard Harris was drinking him under the table.

The music modulates into a major key, the first of about 2,495 key changes to appear, where we get hit full on with the song's controversial (and really depressing) chorus. Harris describes MacArthur Park as a place that melts away when the sun goes down while flowing with green cake icing (no, I did not type that wrong, either). This leads to the infamous refrain where "someone left the cake out in the rain." Harris is beside himself since it took him so long to bake the damned thing and he'll "never have that recipe again . . ." (Webb has spent the rest of his life regretting he ever wrote those lyrics.)

But it's only just beginning. The music modulates again and we're into a bridge, one that's so long you could span Lake Meade with it. Harris tells himself that there will be "another song for me, and I will sing it," hopefully a song less bizarre than this one. There's mention of warm wine being drunk and never letting anyone catch him gazing at the sun. Then Harris goes on (really, he does) to sing yet another set of verses about worshipful eyes, flowing passions, and rivers in the sky, verses that are so navel-gazing he can see what he ate for lunch.

OK, I'm confused. Is it over yet? Not remotely, and this is why "MacArthur Park" drove so many listeners out of their skulls eventually: It just keeps going and going in pure Rasputin Effect fashion, though not in the typical band-jams-while-guitarist-goes-bananas style of the era. While Harris takes a break, Webb adds (*gasp*) yet another section, a charging orchestral interlude that sounds like the score to a car chase in a Steve McQueen movie. Though it's very well done (lots of complex harmonies and time signature shifts), its very inclusion doesn't make any sense. *Where the hell did this come from*, you ask yourself. *What happened to the soggy cake?* After the orchestra exhausts itself, it's back to the chorus one more time for a reminder of the cake being left out in the rain. Harris changes genders while hitting the last note: "Oh nooooo . . . !"

Why It's Depressing

Besides being as incomprehensible as Sanskrit read in a mirror, "MacArthur Park" bums out the average listener thanks to Harris's overwrought singing (he makes Mandy Patinkin sound like Tom Waits) and, of course, its delirious lyrics. I've always found the wet cake reference dispiriting because it conjures up images of some pathetic sap waiting in the park with a surprise cake for his girl who never shows up. While he waits in vain, the rain starts pouring and the whole thing becomes a frosted mess. Is this what happens? God, I hope not because it's really a stupid image.

Jimmy Webb has spent years both defending and explaining away "MacArthur Park." In a recent interview, he qualified it by saying how psychedelic lyrics were all the rage when he wrote the song, using the Beatles' "I Am The Walrus" as an example (he didn't address the issue of goofy psychedelic lyrics, however). But while it's a gloomy song that lasts longer than the fall of Rome, I feel compelled to defend "MacArthur Park" too. The success of the Beatles' *Sgt. Pepper* album inspired many artists of the era to attempt ambitious musical works and most of them chewed suet a lot worse than Jimmy Webb's. (The Rascals' *Once Upon a Dream* concept album is beyond redemption.) "MacArthur Park" was really more of an audacious experiment that unfortunately has become dated, yet there's something fascinating about it. If you've never heard it, don't deny yourself the opportunity to depress yourself while being incredibly bewildered at the same time.

Final note: "MacArthur Park" has been covered over fifty times by other artists. Glen Campbell's is dismal, Andy Williams's is inexplicable, Waylon Jennings's is a hoot, and the big-band instrumental versions by Maynard Ferguson and Stan Kenton are jaw-droppingly horrible. Interestingly enough, the best rendition I've ever heard of "MacArthur Park" is Jimmy Webb's own solo piano and vocal version from his 1996 CD *Ten Easy Pieces*. His serviceable voice and superlative piano playing, along with the absence of orchestration, lift the song out of the pomposity pile and breathe new life into it (the entire album is excellent). Plus, hearing him sing his own lyrics about the cake in the rain makes for good, shameless fun.

Don't Cry Out Loud

Performed by Melissa Manchester
Released 1978 (No. 10 in the US)
Performed by Elkie Brooks
Released 1978 (No. 12 in the UK)
Written by Peter Allen and Carole Bayer Sager

BREAK-UP SONGS have long been a staple of pop music since they're guaranteed to have an audience. Most of them contain all the elements found in an ill-crafted depressing song, which is why the competition for the most debilitating ones can be fierce. Though artists like Richard Thompson and Joni Mitchell are rare, there are plenty of songwriters capable of conjuring up busloads of depressing musical bilge at a minute's notice. One of the best is Carole Bayer Sager.

For my money, few are as gifted at writing gilded schlock as Ms. Sager. A lyricist of uncompromising mediocrity, she has given life to scores of bad pop songs beginning with the Mindbenders' 1966 hit "Groovy Kind of Love" when she was just twenty years old. Since then, she's managed to win an Oscar, a Grammy, a Tony, and two Golden Globes for her songs, leading her to be inducted into the Songwriter's Hall of Fame. Her crowning achievement was winning the 1986 Song of the Year Grammy for the unbelievably banal AIDS anthem "That's What Friends Are For," where she was lionized for writing lyrics like "keep smiling, keep shining . . ."

How does she do it? Quite simply, Carole Bayer Sager has a mercenary knack for hooking up with seasoned composers who cheerfully outfit her leaden lyrics with slick musical backings. She even married her two best collaborators, Marvin Hamlisch followed by Burt Bacharach, before casting them aside for Robert Daly, the former CEO of Warner Bros. Another songwriting partner of hers was the late talented Aussie performer Peter Allen, with whom she wrote several compositions, including the sentimentally cryptic "Don't Cry Out Loud." Singer/pianist Melissa Manchester scored a top-ten hit in 1978 with this numbing number while highlighting many of the elements that made it a classic depressing song: steadily rising melody line, pretentious key change, what-could've-been lyrics, and overblown orchestration that includes a baroque trumpet figure that wanders in from some queen's coronation.

The Song

"Don't Cry Out Loud" begins with a pensive chorded piano figure, the same one that has worked its way into the score of every Broadway musical since *A Chorus Line*. I'm not sure when the sophisticated harmonies of George Gershwin and Jerome Kern were usurped by composers aping "Hey Jude," but I think Andrew Lloyd Webber is behind it. Anyway, Ms. Manchester calmly tells us about a girl (called Baby) who "cried the day the circus came to town." She wants to be part of the circus, we learn, because they always have the best parades and she doesn't want any of them passing by her. So Baby jumps headfirst into the circus after she "painted on a smile," which leads her to take up with "some clown." (Circuses have clowns, you see.) Soon she's dancing on the high wire without a net. Got all that?

The circus in question here is a metaphor for relationships—or maybe it really is a circus because there's a fair amount of elephant dung lying around in this song. Baby is working without a safety net because she's hooked up with a guy in a fright wig who scares the crap out of little kids. This girl clearly doesn't understand that there are few things more terrifying than shacking up with a clown. Clowns leave greasepaint on the sheets and throw pies at inopportune times. So Baby's disillusionment over losing beloved Bozo is the opportunity to talk some sense into her. This is the circus, Ms. Sager reminds her, and if you want to survive, then "don't cry out loud. Just keep it inside, learn how to hide your feelings." I'm not really sure what that line means other than most men get yelled at for doing it.

The next thing we know, the big top has come down. Baby has since fallen off her wire to discover her dreams scattered among the litter of the departed circus. (I'm back in the metaphor again so bear with me.) The love she had for her clown, a "different kind of love" as it's described (ick), has been left behind in the sawdust. Evidently, the clown dumped her for the bearded lady. Still, Baby will survive because she learned from the best, that being Carole Bayer Sager. She tells her to "fly high and proud" and cherish how you "almost had it all." The orchestra kicks in, punching its way to the mandatory overblown modulation while Ms. Manchester takes the melody for a walk in the clouds. The baroque trumpet that plays counterpoint to her soaring soprano is Elizabethan cheese at its finest.

Why It's Depressing

I had to listen to this song more than a few times before I deciphered the whole circus shebang, likely because circuses went out as culturally relevant entertainment on the day *Star Wars* was released. But when I imagine the naïve, heartbroken Baby shuffling past the discarded peanut bags and dancing poodles, I find a lot of depressing aspects to "Don't Cry Out Loud." Knowing that Baby got screwed-up by something as archaic as a circus only confirms that there ain't a whole lot to do in her hometown. If she can't handle the stress of a Barnum and Bailey metaphor, God knows what would happen to her if she ran off to New York City. She'd either be laughed out of Jean Georges or accidentally cast in an Abel Ferrara movie as a gun-wielding hooker.

While Melissa Manchester's rendition of "Don't Cry Out Loud" is the most famous, others have covered it. The most successful is Peter Allen's version, where his reedy tenor and relaxed delivery makes for an easier time than Ms. Manchester's, who approaches the song the way a leaf blower approaches a candy wrapper. Diana DeGarmo, the 2004 *American Idol* finalist, recorded a version that is too slavish compared to Manchester's to be taken seriously; it's less a remake than a color Xerox. The most perverse, though, is Liza Minnelli's total wig-out rendition from her 2002 live album *Liza's Back*. There are no words that can describe how much Liza absolutely destroys this song, eee-NUN-see-A-TING to a hellish degree while phrasing so far behind the orchestra, she's in a different time zone. She also deliberately mixes up the lyrics. "Cry out loud," she bellows, "Don't learn how to hide your feelings." As the song is part of a medley, her version is short, under two minutes, and this is unfortunate because the evil side of me would love to hear a full unabridged performance of "Don't Cry Out Loud" from Liza Minnelli. It would offer plenty of memorable bleakness for the serious listener. If anything, it would give you, the listener, ample opportunity to "cry out loud," thereby defying the dime-store advice of Ms. Sager.

In the Year 2525
(Exordium and Terminus)

Performed by Zager and Evans
Released 1969 (No. 1 in the US and the UK)
Written by Richard Evans

A BLEAK TALE about the future, "In the Year 2525" has the honor of being an even worse "cautionary" song than Barry McGuire's awful "Eve of Destruction." The number 2525 in the title probably stands for the IQ of the two heartland hippies who sang this depressing piece of shit, with Zager having 25 and Evans having 25. Incredibly, the song went to number one in July 1969 for over a month, which probably had something to do with the brown acid everyone was warned about at Woodstock.

Denny Zager and Richard Evans were two Nebraska-born singer/songwriters who played together in a group called the Eccentrics during the early 1960s. Evans quit the band in 1965 but reunited with Zager three years later and they began recording together. One of the tunes the duo put down on acetate was a sci-fi–themed ditty Evans had written years earlier entitled "In the Year 2525." The lyrics were listings of futuristic consequences that sounded like Evans had thumbed through an Isaac Asimov novel while waiting in a grocery store checkout line. They recorded the song in Texas in 1968 for Truth, a small record label that distributed it locally. The wretched single was destined for blessed obscurity until RCA grabbed it and tossed it like a grenade into a US market that was still reeling from the Kennedy/King assassinations, urban riots, and Tiny Tim. With the future looking so bad, "In the Year 2525" captured the zeitgeist of the moment and it hit number one in both America and England. The single stayed at the top of the US charts for six weeks (three weeks in the UK) until repeated listenings made the populace furrow their collective brow and mutter, "Wait a minute. This song blows."

The Song

I suspect Richard Evans was listening to Del Shannon's great classic "Runaway" while writing "In the Year 2525," as both songs are built around the same descending minor chord pattern. But while Shannon had the ingenuity to add a catchy chorus, Evans never went any further and thus he and Zager simply hammer on a downward chord progression over and over until the music resembles two furniture movers carrying a wardrobe down a flight of stairs.

The song begins pretentiously with Zager and Evans striking each chord individually while they describe what life will be like in the year 2525, as if that's a burning concern of anyone's: (*praaannn-nng!*) "In the year 2525 . . ." (*praaannn-nng!*) ". . . if man is still alive . . ." (*praaannn-nng!*) . . . if woman can survive . . ." (*praaannn-nng!*) ". . . they will find . . ." What they'll find is that they have to wait another 1,010 years to see what happens.

The music sluggishly kicks into a medium-slow tempo while these soothsayers tell us about the year 3535 when the first sign of future shock is revealed: Everyone has to take a pill in order to think and converse. Christ, I do that now; it's called Prozac. Now we have to wait another 1,010 years for something else to happen.

Life really starts to reek in the year 4545. We no longer need our teeth or eyes because there won't be anything to eat and "nobody's gonna look at you" anyway. Question: If we don't have eyes anymore, how can we look at each other in the first place, you paisley butterheads? Another 1,010 years . . .

It's now the year 5555. Our limbs aren't needed anymore because whatever work that needs to be done, a machine will do it for you. Like anyone's going to complain about that? Besides, Luddites have been screaming about this since Eli Whitney invented the cotton gin. All of this is somehow lost on Zager and Evans as they've now carried us into the year 6565. Horrors, now babies are being conceived in "the bottom of a long glass tube." What's next? Music will be composed on computers?

The song's first real catastrophe happens during the sixth stanza: Zager and Evans run out of words that rhyme with "five." That's the only reason they break the time sequence and travel to the year 7510. Now God has stepped into the picture, clearly upset that these two have been griping about the past 5,000 years: "Maybe He'll look around Himself and say, 'guess it's time for Judgment Day.'" I for one wholly support the unleashing of the Apocalypse—anything to make Zager and Evans stop singing. A thousand years later, in the year 8510, the Lord is still drumming His fingers on His throne while contemplating what to do, what to do. Zager and Evans theorize that He's either going to be pleased with mankind or start over from scratch.

Zager and Evans run out of words that rhyme with "ten" and pull us into the year 9595, wondering if man will still even be around. By this time, they've changed key three times (the song steadily modulates upward in half steps) while exhausting the patience of a ground sloth. After 10,000 years, they warn us, mankind will cease to exist, having been driven to mass suicide from listening to this song. But that doesn't stop them from starting all over again. "In the year 2525 . . ." they sing as the track fades, the most auspiciously timed ending to a song ever.

Why It's Depressing

The biggest enemy of any futuristic work is the future itself. Schools stopped teaching George Orwell's novel *1984* when 1984 actually rolled around because its vision didn't jibe with the reality. If "In the Year 2525" was the manuscript to a science-fiction novel, it would've been torched long before it reached the transom. Why read a book where something happens once every ten centuries? But we don't have to wait until the year 2525 to know that Zager and Evans get everything wrong from the very start. The two come across like a pair of hack prophets, similar to the Chicken Littles who ran around predicting worldwide chaos as Y2K loomed. Most of the predictions in "2525" have long been implemented into society anyway, and we're all still here.

In hindsight, even publicity photos of Zager and Evans make one suspect their protest song image. They looked like the kind of hippies who might wash up on the shores of a *Gilligan's Island* episode, with their dialogue supplied by former writers for Sid Caesar. It's the interminable caterwauling of these Nostradamus wannabes that sends the listener into a deep funk while the arbitrary key changes do nothing to deflect the music's sonic drone. In short, "2525" sounds far gloomier than it actually is, but it's more than gloomy enough, which is the goal of every depressing song.

Same Old Lang Syne

Performed by Dan Fogelberg
Released 1981 (No. 9 in the US)
Words and Music by Dan Fogelberg

I'M TRYING to think of a wimpier rocker than Dan Fogelberg but can only come up with . . . Dan Fogelberg. A poor man's Jackson Browne (he even looks like him on his early album covers), Fogelberg blazed a mellow trail in the 1970s and 1980s, leaving behind some of the most mawkish tunes ever sung by a white man. His sappy ballad "Longer" will send a komodo dragon into diabetic shock and there isn't a department store anywhere that doesn't have that cringe-inducing song playing overhead while you're shopping for clothes. But the one Fogelberg tune that always sends me plunging like the NASDAQ is his depressing chance encounter tale "Same Old Lang Syne," which is an even worse song than "Longer" because, well, it's longer than "Longer." I know it's played more often as I've heard it in Macy's, Bloomingdale's, Robinsons-May, Saks, and Mervyn's. Hearing Dan Fogelberg songs reminds me of buying socks.

"Same Old Lang Syne" comes from his 1981 album *The Innocent Age*, a two-disc set that generated four Top 20 hits and established Fogelberg as the most sentimental man in show business. Though a talented multi-instrumentalist, he has a penchant for writing songs that gush so much emotion, you wonder how many times can he wear his heart on his sleeve without going into cardiac arrest (sample lyric from "Longer": "we'll fly through the falls and summers with love on our wings . . ."). With "Same Old Lang Syne" he milks the sentiment for all it's worth while describing a surprise encounter with an old girlfriend that is so uneventful, you wonder why he even bothered to sing about it.

The Song

Fogelberg opens "Same Old Lang Syne" in a grocery store (note: This is a bad location to set any song) where he spies an old flame doing some last-minute shopping on Christmas Eve. "I stole behind her in the frozen foods," he sings (note: This is an even worse location), before touching her on the sleeve. Recognizing him, she goes to hug him and ends up dumping her purse out on the floor, to which "we laughed until we cried . . ." (note: No woman thinks spilling everything out of her purse is funny). The action then moves to the checkout stand where the two of them go, chatting away while their groceries are "totaled up and bagged" (note: Who gives a flying Frito?). Fogelberg then realizes that he and his ex-girlfriend have already run out of things to talk about so they stand awkwardly together "as the conversation dragged" (note: This is understandable).

Not exactly "Tangled Up in Blue," is it?

Most of us in similar situations would hightail it out of there with the old it-was-so-good-to-see-you exit line. But Fogelberg has several verses left so things just get more dismal. The two of them decide to go get a drink and catch up but, unable to find an open tavern, they buy a six-pack of beer at a liquor store "and we drank it in the car" (note: You shouldn't have left the frozen foods section). During the chorus, Fogelberg has them toasting each other while trying "to reach beyond the emptiness but neither one knew how." You could recap the interesting moments of this reunion in the time it takes to light a match.

At this point, even the most patient of souls would bail out of the situation, but Fogelberg opts to prize some information out of her. We learn that she's married to a successful architect who she no longer loves (*"those blueprints are so . . . boring!"*). She openly admits it, too: "She didn't like to lie . . ." Great, we think, finally something intriguing is happening. They're in a car together, it's night, they're drinking, and she's bored with her husband. So what does Fogelberg do? He compliments her blue eyes. "I wasn't sure if I saw doubt or gratitude," he sings (note: You saw doubt, Dan, and lots of it).

The woman tells him how she always sees his albums in the record store and congratulates him on his success (note: Wanted to make joke about used Fogelberg LPs in sale bins but felt it was too obvious). He nods, telling her how the traveling can be rough but "the audience was heavenly" (note: Attention Fogelberg fans—you're heavenly). They toast each other again during the chorus and then realize the beer's gone, they've run out of things to talk about, and he hasn't made a move on her. With that, they say good-bye to each other "and I watched her drive away." He's left standing in the parking lot "with that old familiar pain" as the snowfall turns to a rainy mess around him. Then, a curious thing happens. A soprano sax played by post-bopper Michael Brecker comes in and tweedles away distractedly while Fogelberg looks around him trying to find where he put the ending to this song. It sounds like a Kenny G tune tacked on by accident. It finally stumbles to a close, though it takes a full minute to get there.

Why It's Depressing

No matter how plaintively Fogelberg sings, how eloquent the piano accompaniment, or how wafting and soaring the melody during the chorus, it doesn't change the cold fact that nothing happens in this song. You have two people who once dated sitting in a car drinking warm beer while trying not to bore each other to death. Meanwhile, it's Christmas Eve and they had nothing else better to do than buy groceries at the local Food Mart.

There's no cuckolding, no sex, no quickie feel, no sudden flee for the border together, just a big-time rock star and his old girlfriend awkwardly complimenting each other's eyes. "Same Old Lang Syne" has a noticeable amount of lyrical filler, too. How important is it to mention the food being "totaled up and bagged"? I know he needed a rhyme to go with "the conversation dragged," but he could've done better than that. How about "her breasts were perky, they didn't sag" or "I told her I was rich, oh how I bragged?" Fogelberg fans probably find this song moving, and I've no doubt he wrote about an occurrence that happened to him. I myself have had similar mini-reunions with women I'd known in the past and found them just as banal and anticlimactic as the one Fogelberg experiences in "Same Old Lang Syne." The only difference is I didn't write a freakin' song about it.

The Rose

Performed by Bette Midler (taken from the film *The Rose*)
Released 1980 (No. 3 in the US)
Words and Music by Amanda McBroom

PLINNNG PLINNNG plinnng plinnng plinnng plinnng . . .
Whenever you hear the legato tones of a piano playing the
same note repeatedly at the beginning of a song, turn and run for
your life. A piano ballad of puke-retching proportions is oncoming. I cannot emphasize this enough because Ray Charles
and Nat King Cole did not triumph over handicaps and racist
indignities just to have their instrument of choice be used as a
glockenspiel.

Plinnng plinnng plinnng is the opening to the insufferably
depressing song "The Rose," the theme to the 1979 Bette Midler
movie of the same name. In the film, the Divine Miss M played
a Janis Joplin-esque rock singer who finds fame and fortune but
not the love she seeks, so she falls into booze and drugs. The
movie ends with Midler's character dropping dead in front of
thousands of fans during a concert. As her manager slowly walks
across the stage toward her (too slowly when you consider his
sole source of income just died), you hear *plinnng plinnng
plinnng plinnng . . .* It's all very manipulative, designed to make
the tears well up and the nose sniffle even if you can see her
death coming from a mile off. The song plays over the closing
credits, with dewy metaphors and self-pitying reflections on love
drenching you like acid rain. "The Rose" was released as a
single, going to number three in America, and it remains Bette
Midler's biggest-selling hit. While I wholly acquit Ms. Midler for
her role in its creation (she didn't write it, performs it expertly,

and is great in an otherwise mediocre film), it doesn't change the fact that "The Rose" is a maudlin, depressing song that comes out smelling like something other than a rose.

The Song

Plinnng plinnng plinnng goes the piano, *grinnd grinnd grinnd* go the teeth, and we're off and crawling. After a pause so pregnant it's having triplets, Bette begins quietly describing how some people say love "is a river that drowns the tender reed." I've been a part of several conversations about love in my lifetime and can say without hesitation I've never heard anyone say that it's a river that drowns reeds. I've heard how love hurts, love stinks, love is a battlefield, love is like oxygen, but a river that kills plant life? That's a new one.

Often the reason song lyrics go bad is because the writer is so locked into a particular word, he or she relies on stilted phrases just to stay with the rhyme scheme. In "The Rose" we need the "reed" because it rhymes with "seed." And indeed, "seed" is key so follow my lead. See? As the love metaphors keep coming with Bette tossing them out like fish to a seal, we hear how love is a razor ("bleed"), love is a hunger ("need"), until the final refrain where love is "a flower, and you its only seed . . ." See how much trouble we had to go through just to get to here?

The entire time, the *plinnng plinnng plinnng* of the Steinway goes on, on, on. Finally, whoever's holding the gun to the pianist's head falls asleep and the *plinnng plinnng* ends. Alas, it's replaced with the chords from Neil Young's "After the Gold Rush" and Bette takes us into the ultra-dispiriting second stanza of "The Rose" while overdubbing her own harmony vocals: "The heart afraid of breaking," she sings, "never learns to dance." A breaking heart that won't dance? Again, that's a new one but it serves the next line in which love is a "dream afraid of waking" so it never takes a "chance." This is how it works: Find one word and lamely rhyme your way toward it.

More misery-clad musings appear, including souls that never live because they're too afraid of dying (how often has that been used?) along with the hoary life-on-the-road-is-hard-for-us-rock-stars lament, filled with nights that are "too lonely." All this brings us back to the seed metaphor, which is buried under the winter snow but "with the sun's love," as Bette sums it up, "in the spring becomes the rose." The piano trails off and the song ends with a final *plinnng*.

Why It's Depressing

The public's first introduction to "The Rose" was hearing it over a scene featuring Bette Midler's dead body. That's about as melodramatic a visual as you can get and it only complicates matters that her manager is standing nearby with his hands on his hips, shaking his head. (Go rent the movie if you don't believe me. The guy should be freaking out.) The music is just earnest folk guitar played on a piano and, as much as I like minimal production, I wouldn't have minded if the bonehead who played the guitar solo on the Carpenters' "Good-bye to Love" had wandered in and cut loose. At least it would have livened things up a bit.

But what really sends me to aisle nine to shop for razor blades is the song's disturbing air of Songwriting 101. The melody is so basic it sounds like it was assembled from an instruction book ("insert note C into line A . . ."). And how else to explain the soppy lines about drowning reeds, aching needs, and souls that bleed other than they all rhyme with "seed," the same seed that's buried under the snow. (I'm not sure what thirteen-year-old girl's diary the songwriter plagiarized these lyrics from, but I hope she at least got a royalty check out of it.) Adding to the misery is how to this day there's a high school variety show going on somewhere featuring a pair of teen sopranos shakily harmonizing their way through "The Rose" while their parents sit in the audience dabbing their eyes. (Trust me, I've seen it.) "The Rose" is morbid sentimental pap that further stains the reputation of the piano while tempting us to grab the rose so we can flail our bare skin with its thorns.

Mandy

Performed by Barry Manilow
Released 1974 (No. 11 in the UK, no. 1 in the US)
Performed by Westlife
Released 2003 (No. 1 in the UK)
Words and Music by Scott English and Richard Kerr

AS THE SONG responsible for putting Barry Manilow on the map, "Mandy" has a lot to answer for. This overwrought ballad, still saddled with an urban myth (you know what it is, right?), gave the former jingle writer and Bette Midler music director his first number-one hit and set the course for more egregious musical crimes such as "I Write The Songs" and "Copacabana." Although it's not nearly as bad as those two Stuka bombers, "Mandy" deserves a place in the pantheon of depressing songs because of the way he keeps kicking himself for sending poor Mandy away (plus it changes key). The song is even more dispiriting if you can imagine that the urban myth attached to it is true.

For those readers bemused beyond comprehension, let me explain. Following the 1974 release of "Mandy," a rumor surfaced that the song was about Manilow's pet dog. The story went that the dog was loyal to a fault until one fateful day when he coldly sent her packing. Manilow was later wracked with guilt and poured out his anguish in a song he wrote about her: "I sent you awaaay, oh Mandy . . ." This myth has had legs for three decades now and many still believe it.

I was always skeptical about the story, if only because I knew Barry Manilow didn't write "Mandy." Determined to get to the bottom of this, I tracked down the origin of the Mandy myth (which shows you how pathetic my life is that I'm spending time corroborating thirty-year-old Barry Manilow rumors). Allegedly when "Mandy" was a hot single, reporters supposedly kept pestering Scott English, the song's lyricist, to reveal who Mandy was. Frustrated from being harassed, he went into a snit and told a British reporter, "Mandy was my dog, and I sent her away, OK? Now buzz off!" Unfortunately, the reporter worked for one of London's notorious tabloids and English's rebuke was printed as fact, slowly attaching itself to Manilow over the years.

I guess this is plausible, though I'm trying to think of the last time the paparazzi went out of their way to hound a song lyricist. I mean, who cares? We're not talking Angelina Jolie here. I much prefer the dog myth anyway, because if you can picture Barry Manilow cruelly abandoning a loyal dog out in the rain, "Mandy" will really depress the hell out of you.

The Song

The best way to describe "Mandy" (if I must) is like this: It's a Carole King song with lyrics written by someone who thinks Carole Bayer Sager is the bee's knees. Manilow's piano intro to "Mandy" alone sounds King-esque, as if he'd spent a year listening to her *Tapestry* album on a loop. Barry looks back on his life where the rain was "cold as ice." Images of faces in windows and late-night weeping cloud his mind until the morning comes. It's quite an achievement to work in shadows, icy rain, and "cryin' in the night" within the first set of verses, so we can be assured there's more pathos to come. The sight of happy people passing Barry on the street triggers memories of Mandy, dear sweet housebroken Mandy . . . oh, right, she's not a dog. Start over. Dear sweet loving Mandy who came to him and gave until she couldn't give any more until, Manilow sings, "I sent you away . . ."

Now he's "caught up in a world of uphill climbing," implying that either every day is a struggle to go on or he lives in the Pyrenees. The song's lyrics are laden with awkward phrases like "the tears are in my mind" and "crying on the breeze," as if the lyricist was taking his symbolism out for a spin. Manilow returns to the emotional chorus once again, the obligatory strings soaring angelically behind him as he resolves it into the relative minor while still beating himself up for abandoning Spot, er, Mandy. "I never realized how happy you made me, oh Mandy . . ."

The required bridge sets us up for a potential BCM but, when it finally arrives, it's mostly a letdown. Manilow steps into a higher key without the usual whiplash effect, though the drummer drops in loud drum accents like he's trying to imitate Hal Blaine's snare shots on Simon and Garfunkel's "The Boxer." The strings swell and Barry mournfully pleads for Mandy to come back, wailing "I need yooooouuu!!! . . ." He remains alone, surrounded by memories of Mandy laughing, playing, and chewing up his wallet.

Why It's Depressing

Though he hasn't had a hit in twenty-five years, Manilow's legions of loyal fans have made him a top concert draw equal to Neil Diamond, and he gets extra points for his musicianship (he's a fine pianist), lack of ego, sense of humor, and ability to wear suits with shoulder pads so big you could land a helicopter on them. Plus, his catalog is unique in that "Mandy" is the only depressing song I know of that gives you the option of deciding how depressed you want to get while listening to it. If you only need to be nominally depressed, take "Mandy" for what it is, a song about a loving girl who Manilow broke up with out of fear of commitment, only to have second thoughts later on.

But if you're really a prick, try this: Put on "Mandy" and start envisioning Barry Manilow as the owner of the sweetest, most adorable puppy in the world, with a waggy tail and eyes as big as saucers. Mandy loves to romp around the Manilow household, jumping up on the piano bench alongside her master and laying her furry little head on his lap. Now picture Barry Manilow picking up little Mandy by the scruff of her neck, going to the door and . . . THROWING HER OUT IN THE STREET! "GET OUTTA HERE, YA MUTT!!" Lost and alone, poor abandoned Mandy wanders the rainy streets alone, winding up shivering in a dark alley, whimpering, wanting only to be loved . . .

See what I mean?

If I Sing About Drugs, People Will Take Me Seriously

Captain Jack

Performed by Billy Joel
Released 1974
Words and music by Billy Joel

THERE ARE few things more boring to me than addict-speak and, when it's put to music, I resist the urge to take hostages. For years, musicians wishing to be taken seriously have recorded songs about drug addiction, assuming the subject's fatalism will garner them critical respect (i.e., *"They can't dismiss me anymore. I just did a song about heroin."*). Billy Joel's "Captain Jack" is one of those songs, a depressing pop-rock epic from his second album, *Piano Man* (whose oft-played title song is another wrist-slasher), that wears out its welcome early on during its junkie-themed storyline.

Having listened to numerous drug songs over the years and studied their critical analyses, I've concluded that they basically fall into two categories:

1. stark
2. harrowing

Music writers use these descriptors alternately when writing about drug songs. What separates the two normally depends on whether the songwriters were themselves addicted. The Velvet Underground's "Heroin," for example, is "stark" because Lou Reed was once an addict. Billy Joel's "Captain Jack" is "harrowing" because he wasn't. Harrowing drug songs are usually more irritating than stark ones since the former try too hard, lacking the tangible experience that comes from shoving a spike into your arm. Recorded in the early 1970s, a live bootleg recording of "Captain Jack" became an underground FM radio hit, unbeknownst to Billy Joel, who had fled to the West Coast to escape a bad recording contract. The song's notoriety earned him enough recognition to snag a new record deal and his career was under way. The only reason Billy Joel still performs "Captain Jack" is likely out of obligation because, to his credit, even he can't stand it. Joel has admitted in interviews that he's somewhat embarrassed by "Captain Jack," noting his own immaturity when he wrote it while in his early twenties.

The Song

As depressing drug tunes go, "Captain Jack" is arguably the slickest. It begins pretentiously with a baroque figure on a pipe organ before slamming into Billy Joel's trademark pop piano chords, which underpin the verse sections until a clever modulation (there are good ones) takes the listener into a soaring chorus. The music to "Captain Jack" isn't bad at all; you could drop it whole-cloth into a production of *Rent*, which isn't saying much. It's when the lyrics kick in that you start counting the hairs on your arm.

The narrative to "Captain Jack" reworks the template of Samuel Beckett's *Waiting for Godot*, except Godot shows up in the form of the drug dealer whose name graces the title. What's odd is how Billy Joel makes the unbelievably nervy choice to sing this song entirely in the second person so that its drug addict protagonist is you: a bored, affluent slacker living with your parents in a dull burg outside New York City, probably in New Jersey. (I've never been to New Jersey but I'm told readers from New York will think this is funny.) You eventually change into your tie-dyed jeans and head into Greenwich Village to stare slack-jawed at other addicts and guys in drag while waiting for Captain Jack to arrive to give you a little push.

"Captain Jack will get you high tonight," Billy wails during the song's catchy chorus, "and take you to your special island." The next evening, you sit in your room chronically masturbating (oh please) before heading back into the Village again, this time wearing "new English clothes" to wait around for Captain Jack to arrive again. To pass the time, you pick your nose. You this, you that . . . OK, Billy, I get it. I'm pathetic.

As the song drones on and on, Joel unloads more dismal verses describing your lousy life, including listless road trips with no destination, boring make-out sessions in the parking lot with your dumb-ass girlfriend, your dad floating facedown in the swimming pool. (Wait. I have a swimming pool?) But don't worry, "Captain Jack will get ya high tonight . . ." By the song's end, you've been marinated in so much narcotic ennui you're tempted to check yourself into rehab just to get it out of your head.

Why It's Depressing

To say this song is tedious is like saying Bill Gates has a few bucks. First of all, it's lonnnnnng—seven minutes and fourteen seconds to be exact, making it 112 percent of a "Bohemian Rhapsody." But unlike that adventurous piece of art-rock trash with its three separate musical sections, "Captain Jack" is two minutes' worth of music looped together to cover seven minutes' worth of lyrics, each one reminding you over and over again how much of a loser you are.

But the most galling aspect of "Captain Jack" is Billy Joel's decision to sing it in the second person. That's just wrong wrong wrong, like having your plastered brother-in-law stagger up to you at the family barbecue and start the conversation with, "You know what your problem is?" Second person is for cookbooks, birthday cards, and instructions on how to assemble a swing set. It is not for poems, prose, haiku, or lyrical verse, and it's especially not for an interminable drug-fest like "Captain Jack."

Critics have unleashed so much vitriol at Billy Joel over his thirty-year career, you'd think he slept with their wives and poisoned their dogs. The fact that his songs were "celebrated" in the dreadful 2004 Broadway dance revue *Movin' Out* did nothing to enhance his schlockmeister reputation with pundits who refuse to acknowledge his success as a musician and singer-songwriter. That said, "Captain Jack" eats it.

Let Her Cry

Performed by Hootie and the Blowfish
Released 1994 (No. 2 in the US in 1995)
Written by Mark Bryan, Dean Felber, Darius Rucker,
and Jim Sonefeld

FIRST OFF, what do you call die-hard Hootie and the Blowfish fans? Hooters? Blowhards? Fishheads? There were more than enough of them to make a four-piece combo from South Carolina, with the silliest band moniker since Sniff 'n' the Tears, reach multi-platinum status in 1994 with their debut album *Cracked Rear View*. The group's sunny hit "Hold My Hand" was as anti-Seattle as any song could get during the grunge-soaked early 1990s and it helped Hootie and the Blowfish sell 13 million copies of *Cracked Rear View*. Let me repeat that: 13 million copies.

This is significant because that means at least 13 million people bought a CD with "Let Her Cry" on it, along with an additional two million who made the song a top-five single. This could explain the boost in Seagram's stock since 1994, because the only way you can get through this song is to drink yourself blind. While most music fans consider "Hold My Hand" a guilty pleasure akin to eating a patty melt at a vegan restaurant, public serotonin levels dropped like clay pigeons when "Let Her Cry" got airplay and its pretentious music video did the rounds on MTV (back when MTV actually showed music videos).

"Imagine Bill Withers fronting the Eagles," Hootie and the Blowfish proudly say to describe their music, prompting fans to nod in approval while wondering who in the hell is Bill Withers. Critics have disliked the group ever since they broke big because they came across like four post-college guys in a bar band (which they are) who had the utter gall to outsell Nirvana. Worse, none of them were hooked on drugs (musicians, take note: If you want critics to take you seriously, develop a heroin addiction). So for all their bucolic stability, what demented muse inspired them to record "Let Her Cry"?

The Song

I'm always suspicious of songs with the word "cry" in their title because I feel like I'm expected to have a specific reaction to it. Namely crying. Johnny Ray did the classic "Cry" back in 1953 and pretty much carried the whole go-ahead-and-weep concept as far as it could go. "Let Her Cry," however, goes through so many sobbing permutations it ends up with everyone crying: the girl in the song, lead vocalist Darius Rucker, the rest of the band, the session organist, the studio engineer, and God knows who else. The song starts with Rucker wearily strumming his acoustic while introducing us to the 110-pound anchor around his neck, that being a girlfriend who's an alcoholic. Or a drug addict. Or both. I mean, who really cares? "She sits alone by a lamppost," Rucker tells us, "tryin' to find a thought that's escaped her mind . . ." When she eventually does find it, we learn that it's this: She loves her dad the most but "Stipe's not far behind." I'm assuming the reference is to R.E.M.'s Michael Stipe and I cannot imagine this is something that swells him with pride ("*Look everyone, I just got name-dropped in a Hootie song*"). Rucker runs his hands through the girl's hair and assures us he doesn't mind that she's sitting plastered out on the sidewalk.

He's lying, of course. It's the old in-denial dodge. Or maybe he truly doesn't care, in which case he and his Blowfish would have no reason to continue the song, thereby saving everyone a lot of aggravation. But, no, Darius is just getting started. "Just let her cry," he advises us, saying how the tears should fall like rain.

(God, that simile again?) This is the beginning of all the crying that goes on during this song.

The rest of the band comes in, sounding like they're trying to break into "Hold My Hand," since both songs have the same number of chords. Rucker is into the next sorry chapter, however, where he wakes up the next morning to find she's gone. Instead, he sees a note from her saying "maybe I'll be back someday . . ." Either this chick is really wasted or somebody didn't double-check the lyrics because a phrase like "I'll be back someday" always occurs at the end of a song, not one quarter of the way into it. Even Frosty the Snowman knows that.

Anyway, we're back to the chorus again and damn if she's not still crying. Go ahead and let her cry, Darius repeats, saying again how the tears should fall like rain. Sorry to go on about this—I know Darius Rucker is no Dylan but couldn't he have come up with a less creaky simile than having tears falling "like rain"? The merry Blowfish, meanwhile, have given up trying to turn the song into "Hold My Hand." Things have gotten so desperate that guitarist Mark Bryan actually plays the guitar solo from, I swear to God, 4 Non Blondes' "What's Up?" But the gloom has only just begun because by the last stanza, all the buckets are kicked over.

He confesses that he tried to leave the night before, and he "cried so much I could not believe . . ." Oh great, now he's crying. And why is he leaving? I thought she already did that. No, she's made good on her promise to see him again someday and has come back (lucky him). To celebrate, she goes to the back of the house "to get high," which prompts Darius to sit down on his couch and cry some more. She's crying, he's crying, the rest of the band's crying, their tears all falling down like, er, rain. As Darius roars through the chorus for the fifth time, it becomes apparent that there's no limit to how upset someone can get.

Why It's Depressing

Did anybody really listen to this friggin' song when it was a hit single? Did you not dive for the tuner button every time "Let Her Cry" came on the radio? There's not enough Xanax in the world to offset the utter cloud of despair that comes with hearing it. As I've stated before, writing a song about addiction can be a slippery slope and with "Let Her Cry," the entire band is on a toboggan ride down K2. The problem is the old "less is more" chestnut, which both Hootie and his loyal Blowfish follow in reverse. The more Darius bellows the song about his crying wobbly gal pal, the less convincing the whole story becomes, and there's nothing worse than a substandard drug/alcohol song. Granted, Rucker's a good singer, but hearing his chesty baritone reminding us over and over how much everyone is crying makes the whole thing rather dreary.

Subsequent Hootie albums haven't sold nearly as well as their *Cracked Rear View* debut. I'm not sure if it's because people are afraid they'll stumble across yet another soul-stealing song like "Let Her Cry" or because they know owning more than one Hootie and the Blowfish album is pretty much redundant. Still, they'll always have "Hold My Hand."

Sam Stone

Written and performed by John Prine
Released 1972

ALMOST thirty-five years after its release, John Prine's "Sam Stone" still serves a purpose. It's the first song of note to feature a drug-addicted combat veteran as its protagonist while reminding us that the Vietnam War was the "bad" war. For those too young to remember, the Vietnam War was a messy little police action that more or less began in 1961 and ended in 1975 with the fall of South Vietnam, the country America was supposed to defend from Communism. It cost 52,000 American lives and the ones who survived came home to see themselves converted into the Sam Stones depicted so bleakly in Prine's song.

John Prine was a former postal worker turned singer-songwriter who Kris Kristofferson championed early in his career. "Sam Stone" remains one of Prine's signature songs and he continues to sing it in concerts today for audiences who prefer their Vietnam vets to be every bit the loser Sam Stone is. Though it's about drug addiction, "Sam Stone" also became Ground Zero for the composite Vietnam vet stereotype that later emerged: a blue-collar psycho with a Fu Manchu mustache who goes bonkers every time a Doors tune comes on the radio.

The Song

A funereal organ gets everything started until a folky acoustic guitar takes over. "Sam Stone came home to the wife and family," Prine begins, in his trademark nasal voice, "after serving in the conflict overseas..." Sam Stone is carrying around shrapnel in his knee, which understandably left him feeling nervous, mainlining morphine on a daily basis. "There's a hole in daddy's arm where all the money goes," Prine sings during the depressing chorus, adding a line about how Jesus Christ died in vain, a strange remark I don't quite understand other than it's the sort of self-pitying sentiment junkies throw around. His days are all ignominy and tedium, living in squalor with broken radios.

Prine's description of Sam Stone's miserable life is quite vivid, which only makes it that much more depressing to listen to. The inertia of the title character rivals that of an Arctic glacier; he only moves enough to tie off a vein and slam home another shot. Meanwhile, the song incorporates literally every drab colloquialism associated with addicts, including monkeys on the back and grass growing around the brain. Images of rainy trailer parks, rusty swing sets, and cars up on blocks can be seen, as well as sad-eyed Kansas girls named Annie who got hitched to said vet right out of high school. After exhausting his pitiful benefits, Sam Stone goes back to work only to be fired for stealing to feed his habit. "The gold roared through his veins," Prine sings, curiously making morphine the most lively aspect of the song. Otherwise, Sam Stone's neglected kids are running around wearing handout clothing while the hours are spent watching him nod off in a chair. (Remember, these are your hours we're talking about.)

As expected, there's no eleventh-hour turnaround in the sad saga of Sam Stone. He's already lost his house to foreclosure and his ghastly visage makes Iggy Pop look like a steroid fiend. Sam Stone is sprawled in his frayed lounger when "he popped his last balloon." He's buried, forgotten, in a flag-draped casket at the local veteran's cemetery next to a dozen other Sam Stones who went out the same pathetic way he did, so we would assume.

Why It's Depressing

On its own, "Sam Stone" is a quietly effective song (though I can't imagine anyone wanting to hear it over and over again). What makes it so depressing is the stereotyped images it helped foster, which led to yet another tragic aftermath of the Vietnam War: all the bad art that's been created. Variations of the Sam Stone character have popped up innumerable times in plays, movies, novels, songs, ballet pieces, pantomimes, and God knows what else, albeit with a different name and pathology. In the tedious David Rabe play *When You Comin' Back, Red Ryder?* he takes a diner full of customers hostage. In the Brian DePalma film *Casualties of War*, he participates in the rape and murder of a Vietnamese girl. He starts fights in biker bars, sits in his backyard at night weeping over his medals, and always (and I do mean always) sees dead people: dead buddies, dead warrant officers, dead North Vietnamese, dead Laotians, dead Cambodians, dead Viet Cong, dead dead dead. Bruce Willis, Ed Harris, Tom Cruise, and Jon Voight among others have chewed the scenery portraying him in movies. None of this is John Prine's fault but the self-flagellating myth that partly sprang from his song has spread so widely that even pre-1975 enlistees who never left Stateside are still assumed to be unhinged from their 'Nam experiences, while ageing survivors of Iwo Jima and Guadalcanal a generation earlier have always slept soundly. Nowadays, Vietnam veterans have had their emotional reputations restored somewhat and, as a result, nobody writes about them anymore.

Anyone wishing to experience the war-addled Vietnam vet image should just listen to "Sam Stone" once and leave it at that. Forget about renting *Platoon* or watching a production of *Medal of Honor Rag* at your local community theater. It's better to be depressed for four minutes than two hours. World

War II gave us *The Naked and the Dead* and *Catch-22*, while Vietnam gave us Country Joe and the Fish albums and Oliver Stone's career.

Thanks a lot, Robert McNamara.

She Hates Me,
I Hate Her

Love Will Tear Us Apart

Performed by Joy Division
Released 1980 (No. 13 in the UK, no. 42 in the US)
Rereleased 1983 (No. 19 in the UK)
Rereleased 1995 (No. 19 in the UK)
Written by Ian Curtis, Peter Hook, Stephen Morris,
and Bernard Sumner

ROMANTIC estrangement has long been a stock theme in the depressing song oeuvre and Joy Division's "Love Will Tear Us Apart" certainly ranks near the top of the bad love pile. Given their moniker, derived from the nickname for Nazi sex slaves, Joy Division explored alienation and disillusionment in their music so frequently that most of their songs are total downers. Joy Division were stalwarts of the post-punk British music scene that came out of Manchester during the late 1970s, a story memorably retold in the 2003 film *24-Hour Party People*. Like their fellow bands from that city Happy Mondays and the Buzzcocks, Joy Division remains largely unknown in the United States except among American rock music critics who relish the group's brief legacy (they recorded for only two years) and the suicide of its singer/lyricist Ian Curtis, a gloomy epileptic who regularly suffered seizures while performing onstage.

The Song

Originally released just weeks before Curtis hanged himself, "Love Will Tear Us Apart" addresses the disintegration of the singer's marriage to his wife, Deborah. It opens with a hard strumming riff (on an electric bass, no doubt) before settling into a monochromatic clang that never lets up. The opening verses address what is clearly a relationship that is in its final weeks. He sings hollowly of dull routines and meager ambitions, where the only emotion each has for the other is pure resentment: "And we're changing our ways," Curtis sings, "taking different roads. Then love, love will tear us apart again." Curtis's trademark was his baritone android-like vocal style and he "delivers" these lines (the word "sings" doesn't apply) with so much flat ennui he makes Jim Morrison sound like Buddy Holly.

All is not right in the Curtis household, with rhetorical questions being asked: "Why is the bedroom so cold, turned away on your side?" The band, unfortunately, is too caught up in Curtis's bleakness to notice that they haven't changed the song's melody line. James Brown used to yell to his sidemen to find the bridge and milk the search for all it was worth. There is no bridge to this song, nor much of a chorus for that matter. We instead learn waaay too much about the misery in Curtis's married life, including how love is the one thing that paradoxically will drive them apart.

By the time the third verse comes around, you can practically see the couple inside their Manchester flat staring at the walls in paralyzed silence, unable to share their feelings anymore. You can also see yourself barging into said flat and suggesting the two just divorce, fer chrissakes, and be done with it. More and more emotional baggage is unloaded in a steady stream until you're wondering if Ian Curtis was ever happy a day in his life.

Everything about "Love Will Tear Us Apart" is vintage Joy Division, all nervous beats and anxious pulses, music you can crank while sulking in the rain in your trenchcoat. But lacking even a bridge, the song never moves beyond the edgy rattle that it begins with, the only respite being the high ethereal keyboard line that echoes the chorus's melody. Eventually the song fades, leaving the listener grinding his teeth while resisting the urge to head to the nearest pub and pick a fight with a waitress.

Why It's Depressing

"Love Will Tear Us Apart" is a favorite of Joy Division fans and, lyrically, an effective assessment of a crumbling relationship. The problem is that the song is a prisoner of its own style, hewing so closely to the post-punk bleakness of the Manchester music scene that it comes across a tad obvious. Joy Division's jittery sound was innovative at the time and audiences pogoed endlessly at their gigs but, overall, their pessimism and lo-fi anxiety becomes exhausting after a while, like reading a book about Caligula while running on a treadmill. Manchester's musical anxieties would reach their zenith with the Smiths a few years later, sealing the city's reputation as the grimmest metropolis in the Western Hemisphere. Ian Curtis was never the sunniest of lads (half his fans came to Joy Division shows just to see if he'd have a seizure), but he was a talented lyricist who died much too young at twenty-three. Verse-wise, "Love Will Tear Us Apart" is a sublimely devastating song but after adding the music and shoving it between such cheerless fare as "Dead Souls" and "Failures" on the album *Substance*, it becomes just another droning addition to all the hopelessness.

You Don't Bring Me Flowers

Performed by Neil Diamond and Barbra Streisand
Released 1978 (No. 1 in the US)
Written by Neil Diamond, Alan Bergman,
and Marilyn Bergman

TO ALL you music critics and historians who keep insisting that the late 1970s was the punk music era, I'm here to tell you how wrong you are. Nobody listened to punk music back then. Nobody bought Ramones albums either, nor the Stranglers, Dictators, Germs, Black Flag, or Fear (they'll vouch for that). They listened to the Bee Gees and bought albums by drones that specialized in middle of the road (MOR) music. Never has a musical genre been so appropriately named because if you drive in the middle of the road, you'll eventually die in a head-on collision.

Most of us can readily identify MOR music. It's what Satan pipes into the Seventh Circle of Hell to torment burning souls. It's Billy Joel singing "Just The Way You Are." It's Faith Hill and Shania Twain singing country songs that aren't remotely country. It's Anne Murray singing anything. It's Michael Bolton destroying anything. It's white people's music listened to in escrow offices and chiropractors' waiting rooms. It's most definitely the Neil Diamond/Barbra Streisand duet "You Don't Bring Me Flowers."

The song went to number one in the US for several weeks and won a Grammy. "You Don't Bring Me Flowers" was literally the biggest song of 1978, if only because of the two eight-hundred-pound gorillas who joined forces to record this spirit-sapping ballad. Prior to working on this book, I had neither heard nor thought about "You Don't Bring Me Flowers" in decades but, as with any great depressing song, I hadn't forgotten it.

The Song

There's no getting around the awkward aspect about "Flowers" that's been missed by listeners over the years: The song was never written to be sung as a duet. Barbra Streisand included the original solo version of "You Don't Bring Me Flowers" on her 1978 album *Songbird*. As if this wasn't depressing enough, someone then got the bright idea to bring Neil Diamond into the studio to rerecord it with her as a duet. Not only was this overkill (as well as overmaim and overmutilate), it was also illogical. The lyrics are clearly from one person's point of view, namely a dissatisfied woman who's bored with the shlub she's living with and wants to leave. How do I know this? Because no self-respecting guy would ever complain about not getting flowers or hearing any love songs.

Few duets feature as much call-and-response as this recording does. After eight bars of piano and cello, Barbra is heard first: "You don't bring me flowers," she whimpers, "you don't sing me love songs . . ." Suddenly, Neil's booming baritone barges in, echoing her complaints about the lack of conversation between them when he comes home at the end of the day. Then it's back to Babs, who remembers how much he used to love being with her. Then Neil again, saying how after sex, as long as it's good for him, he's happy. Then Babs. Then both: "You don't bring me flowers . . ." Never have two musical egos traded verses so frequently on such a laborious song. It's like watching a Ping-Pong match played in zero gravity.

The second stanza is all Neil's, with Barbara adding subliminal obbligato fills. I suspect that she willingly laid out during this section as it contains the worst set of lyrics in the entire song. "It used to be so natural," Neil croons when describing how they always talked about being together forever. "But 'used to be's' don't count anymore," he declares, describing them as things that lay there until they get swept away. When cataloging great moments in Bad Profundity this line absolutely ranks up there next to anything Carole Bayer Sager ever conceived.

Babs takes the third stanza, where she sadly remembers all the things she was taught in the relationship, namely how to laugh and cry. Keep in mind that three people collaborated on this song, yet none of them could steer clear of the old "teach me how to . . ." chestnut. The song eventually crawls to a close with the drifting energy of a heart patient going under anesthesia.

Why It's Depressing

"You Don't Bring Me Flowers" is still the biggest of the many duets Ms. Streisand has recorded over the years, collaborating with everyone from Frank Sinatra and Ray Charles to Bryan Adams and Vince Gill. Having Barbra Streisand sing along with anyone is like parking enforcement inviting SWAT to help them tow a car. Her air-raid siren vocals tend to dominate everything (I don't even want to know about her duet with Celine Dion). There was absolutely no need for Neil Diamond to come into the studio and sing along with her, if only because it doesn't make any sense within the song's context. (I'm quite aware I'm the only person in the world who's studied this song so closely, so stop rolling your eyes.) It's a solo piece, pure and simple.

What I find so depressing about "You Don't Bring Me Flowers," besides the pitiable lyrics, is the utter laziness behind such a blockbuster hit; two titans phone in a performance of a dispiriting song that sounds like it was dashed off in half an hour. The audience at the 1979 Grammy awards went so crazy when Neil and Barbra came onstage unannounced to sing "You Don't Bring Me Flowers," you'd think Christ had just walked out carrying Mohammed in his arms. Both of them were at the height of their recording careers at the time and could've scored a platinum single reading each other's underwear tags. The problem is, they knew that and there's nothing worse than performers knowing that anything they release will sell like street crack. It seemed that they didn't feel inclined to work very hard, choosing a plodding ballad with trite lyrics that neither of them gave fuck-all about. Neil Diamond cut his teeth as a Brill Building tunesmith and penned many good songs for himself and others, but "You Don't Bring Me Flowers" is not one of them.

In the Air Tonight

Written and performed by Phil Collins
Released 1981 (No. 2 in the UK, no. 19 in the US)

THERE ARE songs that stick with us more than others, often not for the best reasons. One that's clung to me like a barnacle over the years is Phil Collins's "In the Air Tonight," arguably the most depressing hit song of the 1980s. For reasons known only to the demented spawn in charge of programming, this grumpy dirge still finds its way onto FM radio playlists and will reliably crawl out of your car speakers like a balding slug at the exact same spot on the highway where your cell phone cuts out. Of all the jugular-slitting numbers gathered in this tome, "In the Air Tonight" is by far the most oft-played on the radio. Everyone's heard it, including the deaf, the Amish, and those rain forest Indians who put pie plates in their lips.

"In the Air Tonight" was the first single from Collins's 1981 debut solo album *Face Value*. He'd long taken over lead-vocal chores for Genesis following the 1974 departure of Peter Gabriel, steering the group away from its nutty epic songs about hogweeds and talking lawnmowers toward a more mainstream pop sound. Horrified, guitarist Steve Hackett fled into the night, allowing Collins to convert Genesis into the world's first high-concept lounge band. While pressing his suits and throwing away Gabriel's old praying mantis outfits, Collins discovered that his wife was having an affair. His outraged reaction resulted in his writing the bitter song "In the Air Tonight," yet another example of the dire consequences of infidelity. His decision to release such a morbid song as a single is not nearly as bizarre as it was for stations to actually play it.

The Song

"In The Air Tonight" gets off to a glum start with electronic beats from a cheapo drum machine that sounds like the Rhythm Genie from one of those 1970s-era Baldwin console organs. (Phil Collins is a drummer; how lazy can you be?) After a distorted guitar slams a chord, a muffled analog keyboard drones into the mix, laying out pads of funereal chords for what feels like a week. Though some find it eerie, I'm not kidding when I say "In the Air Tonight" has the most tedious intro to a hit single ever; it makes the Cure sound like Elvis Costello. Finally (finally!) Collins begins by singing the chorus, "I can feel it coming in the air tonight." This line still bothers me because having heard this song 18,467 times, I already know there ain't nothin' coming. Collins, however, insists he's been waiting for this moment all his life which, if true, just shows he really needs to get out more.

People familiar with "In the Air Tonight" (that being everybody) have always noted the opening set of verses where Collins coldly sings, "if you told me you were drowning, I would not lend a hand." While he was simply voicing his displeasure toward his estranged wife about her affair, I recently discovered— and I swear I'm not making this up—that these lyrics have inspired a wide variety of urban myths about their meaning. All of them involve Collins actually watching someone drown (I never said it was an imaginative urban myth). My personal favorite is the version that claims Collins watched someone who watched someone else drown. Impressed, he gave the man front-row tickets to one of his concerts, trained a spotlight on him, and sang "In the Air Tonight" while the bad Samaritan beamed proudly. (I'm going on the record saying that this whacked-out story is far more entertaining than the song is.)

"I was there and I saw what you did . . ." he sings, ordering her to wipe the grin off her face. "It's all been a pack of lies . . ." The backing track creeps along underneath him as he returns to the chorus, reminding us how he's been waiting for this moment all his life. He recalls the first and last time they ever met, referring to either his wife, the man that cuckolded him, or a former Genesis fan who stopped him in the street to ask him why the group blows now. "I know the reason why you keep your silence up," he says, finally adding some timber to his delivery. The internal pain he feels is growing between the two of them. Then (sigh) back to the chorus . . .

Though Collins eventually kicks up "In the Air Tonight" by adding real drums and a hook-filled guitar riff, it's too late. Having run out of lyrics, he falls back on the chorus to remind us again how he feels it "coming in the air tonight." The song ends as drab as it began, with a long-drawn-out fade. It takes forty-five seconds before it finally concludes with Collins raging the whole time about "it" coming in the air tonight, whatever it is. Oh Lord!!

Why It's Depressing

What's always driven the spike into my skull with "In the Air Tonight" is the chorus. There are some dark, interesting lyrics in this song, but they're overwhelmed by Collins's insistence on repeating "I can feel it coming in the air tonight" over and over (and over and over) until it rivals "99 Bottles of Beer" for sheer annoyance. True, repetitious choruses are a staple of pop music, but Phil Collins appears to threaten something that he never makes good on. What's coming? Divorce? Bodily harm? "Sussudio" cranked to ten? We never find out, and what seems an ominous threat comes off like Ralph Kramden yelling, "One of these days, Alice . . . !"

But what ramps up the depression is the oppressive music. "In the Air Tonight" sounds like a prog-rock group playing an MOR song while hoping not to get caught. The song clocks in at five and a half minutes with nearly two minutes being the intro and fade-out. That's a lot of time devoted to musical bookends while the main body is just wall-to-wall ennui, draining and bleak. I'll never understand why "In the Air Tonight" was a single nor why it keeps getting airplay. If he puts one of the urban legends to music, though, let me know.

Brick

Performed by Ben Folds Five
Released 1997 (No. 26 in the UK, no. 6 in the US)
Written by Ben Folds and Darren Jesse

Note: Many people who first heard the Ben Folds Five song "Brick" assumed it was a sad lament to the end of a relationship. They discovered later that it's actually about a couple getting an abortion. My analysis of this song is based on the first assumption, which means it's wholly inaccurate and everything you're about to read is completely wrong. I have indicated where in the text. If you always knew what "Brick" is about, then you'll find what follows bizarre and unnecessary. Please skip to the next song.

IT'S TO THE credit of Ben Folds Five (the group was a trio) that they were actually quite good, often superb, since history has shown us that bands with annoyingly quirky names tend to reek like dead eels. It started back in the 1960s when bands were signed simply because they had trippy monikers (Strawberry Alarm Clock, Peanut Butter Conspiracy, Ultimate Spinach) and continued on through A Flock of Seagulls, Men Without Hats, Butthole Surfers, G'war, ad nauseam. When a group's sole commodity comes from whatever joke, non sequitur, or giggly pun is featured in its name, it's almost a given that its CDs should be used for skeet practice (this is true).

Ben Folds Five was different. Eschewing guitars, turntables, and digital doo-hickeys, the group offered clever off-beat songwriting and a high-energy barrelhouse sound based around the virtuoso piano playing of vocalist/leader Folds. (He has since gone solo, which, if you do the math, makes him Ben Folds

1.66666.) So it is with some regret that I include "Brick," the band's dismal ballad about a teen couple breaking up (this is wrong) to my list of all-time depressing songs. If it had just been an obscure track from one of their albums I may not have cared, but when the evil gods of marketing opted to release it as a single along with an accompanying video, it garnered way more airplay than was ever necessary (this is true).

The Song

"Brick" is the one of those depressing tunes in which nothing of any real interest happens (this is wrong). Repeated listenings to the lyrics yield the same result every time: A guy picks up his girlfriend one morning, bitches, takes her someplace, bitches, waits for her, bitches some more, then brings her back home, still bitching. That's pretty much it (this is true). We never really know what's transpired in between (this is wrong) yet the song's paralyzing gloom still sends us into a dysthymic spiral (very true). All we know for certain is that it's about a young couple who are splitting up (again, this is wrong).

"Brick" features an abulia-wracked piano figure, which Ben Folds bemusedly plays throughout the recording. That it sounds exactly like Bruce Springsteen's "Jungleland" if "Jungleland" were played at half-speed down an octave only confuses matters. (This is true. Piano players, try it. Be amazed.) Did Ben Folds plagiarize? Of course not. Nowadays any slow song built around a solo piano can't avoid sounding like 5,000 other slow songs built around a solo piano* (this is wrong; the number's more like 10,000). Folds wearily begins singing about waking up at six in the morning the day after Christmas so he can drive over to his

---

* It also sounds exactly like the opening guitar figure to Dire Straits' "Romeo and Juliet." (This is true. Guitarists, try it. Be amazed.)

girlfriend's apartment. It's dark, it's cold, nothing's open, blech. Arriving, he finds her "balled up on the couch" and her parents gone. "They're not home to find us out," he adds, making everything sound very intimate (this is wrong).

The next thing we know, they're driving somewhere in numb silence during which he lets us know that, "she's a brick, and I'm drowning slowly . . ." Wow. What young lass wouldn't want this guy for a boyfriend? Who wouldn't want to be awakened at dawn and thrown into a car seat on a freezing winter morning alongside a scowling twerp who thinks you're a brick? Now, the girl's name is being called by someone in a waiting area, likely a dentist for a check-up and tooth cleaning (this is wrong). Meanwhile, Chuckles is sulking in the parking lot, his fists jammed into his coat pockets. He wanders down the street to get her some flowers, thinking four zinnias and some tulips will excuse the fact that he's behaving like a jerk. Once again, "She's a brick and I'm drowning slowly . . ."

So what's going on? You have no idea (OK, you do now, but just play along and pretend like you don't) though we can assume that the two are finished as a couple and want to end things (this is wrong). Weeks later, we find out that "she was not fine," which leads his parents to corner him and say "Son, it's time to tell the truth." They break down and confess: They're no longer going steady (this is completely wrong).

Good, now that we all know what "Brick" is about, teen sopranos who "love this song" can sing it at their high school assembly. (This is a joke. Please don't do it.) The song ends with the guy and girl driving back to her apartment, both of them feeling alone, really really alone. They eventually break up outside her front door. (Wrong.)

Why It's Depressing

If you feel inclined and have hours of time to waste, try to compare how men and women songwriters address deteriorating relationships: Women feel betrayed or unfulfilled, men just want to get the hell out. Women spin gauzy webs of turbulent poetry that they hope will mesmerize an auditorium; men employ simple observations that their dog will understand, i.e., she's a "brick" and that's that. The problem with "Brick" is that it's both musically deadening (Folds's piano playing is really a downer) and lyrically glum, filled with cryptic remarks about bricks and drowning from feeling bored in the relationship (wrong). But because its meaning is somewhat obscure, it took my expert analysis (which is completely wrong) to figure out what the song was about.

In short, "Brick" feels as heavy as its title and there are much better songs that address the demise of young love (if that's what "Brick" is about, which it's not). Ben Folds Five was a great upbeat band (true) and Folds 1.6666 still tours as a headliner (true), but their decision to sing about the disintegration of a relationship (again, false) in such a serious manner is too dispiriting. But at least I was here to explain it.

Ruby, Don't Take Your Love to Town

Performed by Kenny Rogers and the First Edition
Released 1969 (No. 2 in the UK, no. 6 in the US)
Words and Music by Mel Tillis

THERE ARE so many insults and nasty barbs about Kenny Rogers's career that I must desist from joining in on the cat-calling. He's no longer the country music powerhouse he was twenty years ago when he and Barbara Mandrell were Vegas-izing Nashville, and today he shills for a casino in San Diego. Suffice to say, I've never cared for his music, save for "The Gambler," which was a decent song until they made those movies that tried to pass off Linda Evans as a bounty hunter (please). Plus, how long is he going to keep that white sea captain's beard?

If you can imagine this, though, Kenny Rogers used to be a rocker. Maybe not a TV-smashing arena-screaming drive-a-Rolls-into-a-swimming-pool rocker but a rocker none the less. As the bassist/lead vocalist with his group the First Edition, he charted a few light rocking tunes, beginning with the psychedelic "Just Dropped in (to See What Condition My Condition Was In)," which is as hilariously bad as the title would imply. To his credit, he didn't care for the First Edition's harder stuff that the guitarist preferred because he wasn't comfortable singing it, and tried to steer them toward softer country rock-style songs. One of them, unfortunately, was the unbelievably creepy "Ruby, Don't Take Your Love to Town," about a paralyzed war vet with an unfaithful wife. The song, written by Mel Tillis, was one of the

First Edition's biggest hits and, today, it never fails to instill an "ick" reaction from me whenever I hear it.

The Song

"Ruby" starts off cheerily enough, with a *choong chaka choong chaka choong* figure hurriedly played on a snare drum with a damped acoustic guitar strumming in unison. The song's narrator is watching his wife getting all dolled up for a wild night on the town. "You've painted up your lips and rolled and curled your tinted hair," Rogers sings. The woman is Ruby, cold heartless bitch Ruby, who is preening in front of the mirror in full vamp mode as her husband looks on sadly; he asks her if she's going somewhere, knowing the answer is yes. The sun's going down and Ruby's heading for the nightlife, at which the man tells her, "don't take your love to town."

The man, you see, is crippled, the victim of a war wound he got in 'Nam (which Rogers refers to as "that old crazy Asian war" for some reason). Unlike those pot-smoking Commie pinko hippies, he went off without complaint and did his time getting shot at by Charlie. So what thanks does he get? He has to spend every night in his wheelchair watching his rolled-and-curled wife make a fool out of him by hooking up with other men. He admits to her that he's not the man he once was, but adds with a whimper, "Ruby, I still need some company."

Oy vey. By the time you're this far into the song, you feel guilty about even having legs. If this was John Prine's Sam Stone stuck in the wheelchair, there'd be no problem. He'd be too busy nodding off to care about Ruby going out on tramp detail. But this man has all his faculties save his ability to walk, so it's clearly humiliating for him to watch his trashy wife heading out to look for any Wyatt, Bubba, or Billy Bob who can rock her world. The man even tries the guilt approach, reminding her how the doctors say "it won't be long . . . until I'm not around."

Great, she thinks, *you'll kick it and I'll get the life insurance.* God, she's eee-vil.

Though I have no pull with the gods of processing, I've always wished a tape malfunction would've prevented this song from being recorded any further. The absolute worst part of this miserable story occurs during the final stanza when the music drops out to just the skipping snare drum figure. We hear Rogers sing that she's leaving, slamming the door behind her. The crippled man, beside himself with grief and rage, says how he wished he could move just so he could get his gun. You're more than happy to express ship him a .44 magnum to do the deed but, instead, he sits helplessly while gazing at the door. "Oh Ruby, for God's sake turn around," Rogers says in a sibilant whisper. The skipping drum fades off, leaving the poor sap with a cold TV dinner while listening to a car drive off.

Why It's Depressing

Even with its music being so hoppity-skippity, "Ruby" always makes for an unsettling listening experience. It's one of those songs where I have no clue why it was released as a single or why it was a hit. Rogers has described himself as not being a great singer but rather a great storyteller. That may be true, but in the case of "Ruby," it's a moot point because who in their right mind would want to hear this story? Just the visual of an invalid sitting alone in his trailer home while wifey-poo is out catting around trying to pick up truckers at the Stagger Inn is just too depressing to imagine. The guy really needs to take the initiative to roll himself over to the closet where he keeps his gun and start laying down some serious ground rules. What "Ruby" needs is something otherwise unheard of in a depressing song: another set of verses.

The song should end with the man sitting in the dark with a glint in his eye and a 12-gauge pump on his lap. When Ruby finally arrives home reeking of some stranger's Aqua Velva, he flips on the standing lamp, silhouetting him with a surreal backlight. "Hello, Ruby," he says with sneer, pumping a shell into the chamber. There should be a horrified reaction, numerous pleadings, and a final cross-my-heart-hope-to-die promise never to stray again. The next day, the man is suddenly able to get around on crutches while Ruby rubs his shoulders, cooks his steak, and dresses up like Daphne from *Scooby Doo* whenever he demands it. Now that's a "Ruby" I can enjoy.

Horrifying Remakes Of Already Depressing Songs

All By Myself

Performed by Celine Dion
Released 1996 (No. 6 in the UK, no. 4 in the US)
Originally written and performed by Eric Carmen
Released 1976 (No. 12 in the UK, no. 2 in the US)

THERE IS a stock device used in slasher films known as the "false relief." It's when the stalked and terrified heroine hears a scratching noise at a window and raises up the blind only to find an errant tree branch banging against the glass. Sighing with relief, the girl thinks she's in the clear until the machete-wielding killer crashes through an adjacent window a few seconds later and vivisects her. With this in mind, let us revisit the recorded history of "All By Myself." To whit: Eric Carmen leaves the Raspberries to pursue a solo career, and writes a really long ballad about loneliness entitled "All By Myself" based on Rachmaninoff's really long Third Piano Concerto. That's the sound of something scratching on the window. The song becomes an unexpected top-ten hit in 1975. That's the terrified heroine raising the blind. Yet despite its bathos and faux-Russian misery, Carmen's "All By Myself" inflicts no lasting harm on the listener. That's the heroine finding a tree branch banging on the glass and sighing with relief.

Celine Dion doing a remake of "All By Myself" is the deranged killer crashing through the adjacent window.

The Song

At first Celine Dion follows Carmen's song more or less faithfully. "All By Myself" begins with a pinging piano, a device shamelessly used in that other vein-opener, Bette Midler's "The Rose" (see page 81). Celine reminisces about wild younger days when she never needed anybody and how "making love was just for fun." That nobody in their right mind would ever believe Celine Dion spent her formative years deflowering guys indiscriminately is beside the point. Her delivery has already sucked you in, holding you fast until there's nothing to do but wait for the moment when you know she's going to totally lose it. She laments for long-gone friends who are never home when she calls them (trust me, Celine, they're home. It's just that with caller ID, they know it's you calling). On the song's Rachmaninoff-cursed chorus, she mournfully declares: "All by myself, don't want to live all by myself anymore . . ."

Celine confesses to being racked with insecurity while considering love to be "distant and obscure," an emotion that is her only salvation yet remains out of reach. Again: "Allll byyyy myyyy-selll-elf . . ." The chorus, repeated several times throughout the song, is so unrelenting that you can't imagine things getting any worse. But they do, because like any good horror movie, Celine is building the suspense.

In the original version of "All By Myself," Eric Carmen adds a musical "interlude," reworking elements of Rachmaninoff's second piano concerto into a pastiche of Romantic exercises that sound like the 11 P.M. show at the Beethoven Lounge. Celine Dion skips all the classical nonsense, opting instead for the keyboard to work its way through the bridge while she gears up for the surprise assault, beginning with the dreaded BCM.

BCMs, or brain concussion modulations, are a standard element in most 1990s power love ballads and nobody changes key with the force of a hurricane better than Celine Dion. Modulations have been around since Bach was tempering his clavichord, but are used to add color to a composition. Celine's BCMs induce whiplash while letting her demonstrate her ability to shatter tank armor from three miles away. In "All By

Myself," Celine nods to the orchestra, then launches into a BCM that sounds like a DC10 crashing into your house. From this point on, it's Visigoth time and she takes no prisoners, her vocal histrionics surpassing the blood-soaked psychic fury that slaughters the prom-goers at the end of the movie *Carrie*: "DON'T WANNA LIVE ALL BY MYSELF, BY MYSELF, ANYMOOOOOORRRRRRRRRRRE!!!!" she shrieks in her Acadian wail, triggering cataclysms everywhere. By the time the song fades out, the carnage left behind is apocalyptic: Walls have buckled, foundations have crumbled, locusts are unleashed, worlds have collapsed, universes have imploded. Plus, the cable's out.

Why It's Depressing

Celine Dion makes the fatal error of many uber-vocalists by not performing "All By Myself" in its proper context. When recording his original version, Eric Carmen instinctively knew that he wasn't retelling the death of Socrates. Though he overstuffs it with neo-Romantic bloat, Carmen sings with a world-weary timbre that belies any attempt at overt melodrama. Ms. Dion's version, on the other hand, resembles two tectonic plates battling over a continent. Listening to her wrap her Wagnerian pipes around "All By Myself" is like watching a Huey helicopter being used on a fox hunt; it's so out of proportion to the task at hand, it's beyond criminal. True, Celine Dion made her career transforming assembly line power ballads into maelstroms of sound and fury, but her remake of Carmen's song is the audio equivalent of the firebombing of Dresden. In fact, had she been around in 1944, the Allies could've skipped the D-Day invasion and just dropped her off at Omaha Beach with a PA system so she could sing "All By Myself" until the German infantry bayoneted themselves.

Without You

Performed by Mariah Carey
Released 1994 (No. 1 in the UK, no. 3 in the US)
Performed by Harry Nilsson
Released 1972 (No. 1 in the UK and the US)
Performed by Badfinger
Released 1970
Written by Pete Ham and Tom Evans

IT MAY BE a stretch to call it the Hope Diamond of pop ballads but I defy anyone to find a song with more bad luck attached to it than the heart-grinding "Without You." Unlike the apocryphal suicides attributed to "Gloomy Sunday," "Without You" has well-documented traumas as part of its thirty-five-year history, including two suicides, bankruptcy, embezzlement, premature death, divorce, nervous breakdowns, and being a member of Air Supply. What's odd is how those who have served the song the most faithfully were screwed the worst, while the ones who royally butchered it got off with a light slap on the wrist. I take no responsibility for whatever ills befall those who read about "Without You," but if you're overly superstitious, skip this song and move on.

Before we get to Mariah Carey's evisceration of "Without You," let's revisit the song's doomed history. It was written by Pete Ham and Tom Evans, who cofounded the ill-fated rock band Badfinger. Books have been written about the gargantuan tragedies that befell this marvelous group, the first act signed to the Beatles' Apple Records label. Badfinger scored several hits with excellent songs like "Come and Get It" (penned by Paul McCartney), "Baby Blue," "Day After Day," and "No Matter

What," while also backing up George Harrison on his solo albums and performing at the famous Concert for Bangladesh. Along the way, Pete Ham, Badfinger's principal songwriter, and Tom Evans collaborated on a touching song called "Without You." Its chorus was ominous: "I can't live, if living is without you . . ." A minor hit, it appeared on the band's second Apple release in 1970. Then singer Harry Nilsson got ahold of "Without You," slowed it down, added a sparse piano, altered the chorus to "I can't liiiiiiiiive . . . ," and knocked it out of the park, scoring a number-one single in 1972. Nilsson's emotional lump-in-the-throat rendition was such a masterpiece that even Badfinger openly admitted it was far better than their original version. Nilsson had a monster success, Pete Ham and Tom Evans got a fat royalty check, and Badfinger left Apple for a million-dollar record contract with Warner Brothers.

Then it all went bad for the group. Their troubles began when Warner Brothers accused them of "misappropriating" $600,000. Their albums were pulled from stores, tours were postponed, and the group's assets were frozen, effectively bankrupting them. The missing money turned out to be a record company accounting error, but by then it was too late. Pete Ham, a gentle and sensitive soul, was so devastated from the stress of the matter that he committed suicide in 1975, hanging himself. Badfinger disbanded, then attempted a comeback in 1978. By the early 1980s, they were playing bars for tiny fees and ended up stranded in a freezing Wisconsin farmhouse with nothing to eat but a box of crackers and some jam, waiting for their manager to scrape up some work. In 1983, "Without You" cowriter Tom Evans, in an eerie replication of Pete Ham, also hung himself.

As for Harry Nilsson, he never matched the success of his quintessential recording of "Without You." Booze and cigarettes all but destroyed his incredible tenor voice. He kept writing and recording, even doing the score for the Robin Williams film flop

Popeye. By the early 1990s, Nilsson was wracked with diabetes and a weak heart. He was also financially ruined after a trusted assistant embezzled millions of dollars from him, money that was never recovered. He died in 1994 of a heart attack.

Air Supply released a version of "Without You" in 1991, in a rare moment demonstrating that the curse works both ways. Enough said.

The Song

This leaves us with the 1993 remake of "Without You" by Mariah Carey, who used the song for her next single the same way Oppenheimer used uranium to build the A-bomb. Her version mimics Nilsson's practically note for note (as does Air Supply's) right down to the moody piano, tempo reading, and taffy-pulling chorus. "Without You" is one of those numbers that divas like Mariah and her ilk salivate over because it's one of the easiest songs to belt without having to get out of your recliner.

"Well, I can't forget this feeling or your face as you were leaving," she begins, singing in the note-shifting manner of her contemporaries Whitney and Celine, exhibiting the primal impatience of a six-year-old trying to sit through a lecture on grain futures. As the digitally enriched instruments fall in behind her (the drums sound like they were mixed inside the Taj Mahal), Mariah laments "I had you there but then I let you go . . ." and now feels compelled to say how she really feels.

"I can't liiiiiiiiiive, if living is without you," she croons before aping the famous Nilsson version by jumping a whole octave and wailing out the line once again. She then overdubs her voice during the latter half of the song, creating an odd chorusing effect that resembles a flock of mezzo-sopranos diving off a five-story building. By the time she repeats the chorus a second time, she's called in the heavy artillery by adding a bloated choir behind her bellowing "I can't liiivve . . . I, I can't liiivve . . ." The bombast rivals a Roman legion arriving in a Ridley Scott movie, and you wonder how they made room for that many people in the studio. Meanwhile, Mariah has hit every note in a chromatic scale. The only thing that keeps it from Perfect Storm status is that there are no BCMs.

Why It's Depressing

The whole tortured backstory to "Without You" makes it a risky song for anyone to sing because its subtext is as large as the *Queen Mary*. It's a heartbreaking composition, especially when you consider how its composers both left this life bankrupt and humiliated. All of this is lost on Mariah, who basically uses the song for skeet shooting. While the Nilsson version has him holding the pitch of each note like a taut wire, Mariah employs her exasperating faux-gospel technique of toying with the melody like she's dangling a string in front of a cat. I'm not a music fascist by any means, but I wouldn't object to a moratorium being placed on any future recordings of "Without You." Nilsson's sublime version is all the world needs and hearing it being masticated by Mariah Carey or an *American Idol* contestant is in no way a tribute to the two sad young men who died after being crushed by the music industry. Let the song rest in peace—and somebody tell Mariah to please fire the choir.

I Will Always Love You

Performed by Whitney Houston
Released 1992 (No. 1 in the UK and the US)
Re-enty on UK charts 1993 (No. 25)
Originally written and performed by Dolly Parton
Released 1974 (No. 1 on country charts in US)

JUST TO SHOW that I'm not the heartless bastard readers may think I am, I'm refraining from any snarky remarks about Whitney Houston's troubled personal life. I think "How Will I Know" is a great pop/R&B single, her rendition of "The Star-Spangled Banner" is moving, and "All the Man that I Need" is a textbook example of a singer making a great record out of a mediocre song. I think she has a powerful voice and a stunning stage presence. Now let's load up the .38, spin the chamber, bite down on the barrel, and take a look at "I Will Always Love You," shall we?

It's common knowledge that Dolly Parton wrote and recorded "I Will Always Love You" in 1974, and that it was featured in the soundtrack of her 1982 movie *Best Little Whorehouse in Texas*. Quiet and sincere, Parton's original version could bring a lump to the throat of a sword-swallower but the song was never a hit. It lay neglected for several years until Whitney Houston was handed "I Will Always Love You" with orders to reload it for bear. Her version underscores the weepy ending to her hit film *The Bodyguard* where she says good-bye to Kevin Costner. The movie's soundtrack went on to sell 22 million copies worldwide, second only to *Saturday Night Fever*, and the single "I Will Always Love You" was the biggest seller of 1992, the third biggest in 1993, and still one of the ten biggest of all time in both the US and the UK. In short, "I Will Always Love You" was a phenomenon and nothing anyone can say will ever change that.

That said, I'm still compelled to throw myself in front of a moving semi whenever I hear it. For all of you who think I'm exaggerating for hyperbole's sake, I give you an actual line of dialogue from *The Bodyguard*, as spoken by Whitney Houston's character, Rachel Marron, in regard to this song: "I mean, it's so depressing. Have you listened to the words?"

The Song

Whitney Houston has released many power ballads before and since "I Will Always Love You," but none of them fakes you out the way this one does. Unlike Parton's original, with its melancholy acoustic guitars and Floyd Cramer piano, Whitney begins it a cappella. This is significant because she never does that. Normally, the Whitney template involves her waiting for whatever processed nonsense that tracks her songs to settle into place while her producers decide which level of the gospel meter she should hit. But with "I Will Always Love You," there she is, in full solo voice with not a backing track anywhere. "If I should stay," she begins with quiet intensity, "I'll only be in your way." Already I'm suspicious. Where's the Sinn drum? Where's the orchestra pads? Where's the annoying MIDI piano that sounds like a vibraphone on steroids? My word, Whitney's doing this alone and sounding marvelous, too, even if the lyrics are pretty sad. "So I'll go," she sings, "but I know I'll think of you . . ."

At the chorus, however, an acoustic guitar (badly mixed, as usual) and strings start to creep in behind her as she sings "And IIIIII will always love yoooooouu . . ." When the drums and *pling-plong* MIDI piano appear, you realize you've been had. It's shaping up to be another depressing diva power ballad with all the de rigueur elements, including lyrics that get more sentimental while the vocal turns more baroque. Whitney sings how bittersweet memories are all she has to take with her, while her gospel flourishes become more apparent. "I'm not what you need," she insists but "I'll always love you."

An alto sax solos for sixteen bars while Whitney takes a breather. It should be noted that instrumental breaks during power ballads have no purpose other than to allow the singer to prepare for a BCM (see "All By Myself"). When she returns, Whitney wishes joy and happiness and love because it's the last time we'll ever see her until *Waiting to Exhale* comes out. The music takes a deadly pause, and then ... WHAM! A full-on BCM lunges forth, smacking you over the head and stealing your wallet. Whitney goes full tilt into the transposed chorus, working in so many extra vowels while singing "I" and "you" that it sounds like a diphthong festival. The sax wails, the drums pound, and the acoustic guitarist packs up and leaves because who the hell's gonna hear him now? By rights, the song should end with a fade so as not to interrupt Whitney's wailing but they somehow manage to rein everything in, bringing her back down to mother earth where she displays her controlled side once more. She flawlessly hits three consecutive notes on the very last word, in such an unexpected manner it actually sounds (*gasp!*) ad-libbed. Other than the a capella opening, it's the only hopeful moment in the song; the rest is digital dramatics. Worse yet, the MIDI piano finishes it off.

Why It's Depressing

I cannot bag on the lyrics to "I Will Always Love You" because there's really nothing wrong with them. Sure, they're sentimental, maybe even sappy, but they work well in Dolly Parton's version because she sings it in the proper context: wistful and longing. Whitney Houston, on the other hand, makes a royal tragedy out of what's supposed to be a last good-bye. It's really not her fault as I've no doubt the Arista Records bean counters had this in mind, and who can blame them? They made enough money from Whitney's version to buy the souls of a hundred divas just like her. Still, the song is a melodramatic mess of a monster ballad, and the music video for "I Will Always Love You" is one of the worst I've ever seen: Whitney sings while sitting in a chair dressed in a dark suit, her feet apart and her hands clasped together. She looks like a high school basketball coach studying a new point guard. The video alone depresses me because I want to see my Whitney standing before a mike stand wearing a willowy dress, beaming and angelic, i.e., pre–Bobby Brown. She shouldn't look like she's waiting for a job interview.

I'll say this much: I'm likely the only person who's ever wished Whitney Houston had sung the entire song a cappella. It'd be interesting to see the expression of bewilderment on her face when she realizes that she's enjoying herself.

Landslide

Performed by Smashing Pumpkins
Released 1994 (No. 3 in the US)
Performed by the Dixie Chicks
Released 2002 (No. 1 on the Country charts in the US)
Performed by Fleetwood Mac
Released 1976
Words and Music by Stevie Nicks

THOUGH I'VE taken this generation's biggest divas to task for their criminal remakes of older songs, I want to emphasize that it was the way they remade them that I had an issue with. I believe most any song should be open to interpretation and that sometimes a remake will yield better results than the original (see "Hurt" on page 219). Still, there are those select songs that should be left alone because they have a strong tangible connection to the artists who first wrote and sang them like, say, Limp Bizkit's "Nookie." (OK, bad example but you know what I mean.) Sometimes, common sense must take precedence over ego or artistic pretence, and certain luminaries should not be permitted to cover a famous song simply because they think they can do it better. This absolutely applies to Fleetwood Mac's "Landslide," especially when someone like Billy Corgan from Smashing Pumpkins gets ahold of it.

"Landslide" first appeared on Fleetwood Mac's self-titled 1975 album, the one that introduced Lindsay Buckingham and Stevie Nicks to the pop music world. Fans know it as the famous acoustic number Nicks wrote about growing older, and it went on to become a staple of FM radio. "Landslide" has always been useful for Nicks because it helped show the world she wasn't really a witch. It's a beautiful song that still holds up thirty years after its release because Lindsay Buckingham's guitar accompaniment is superb and Nicks left her Zen pen at home when she wrote it.

That's why it was a shock to me when I turned on my car radio and heard some braying nut singing "Landslide" like he was passing a croquet ball through his colon. *Who in God's name is that*, I wondered, while trying to keep from crashing into a light pole. At first I wasn't sure, though the voice sounded irritatingly familiar. Then I realized. It had to be Billy Corgan of Smashing Pumpkins because only he sings like that and only he would have the balls to crucify a mellow gem like "Landslide." Maybe I'm letting my subjective musical tastes color my judgement, but let's be honest here: The Pumpkins' cover of "Landslide" pretty much eats dead crow.

The Song

Things start off fine during the opening of "Landslide." The guitar part is played properly and it sounds like the Pumpkins are making an earnest attempt at doing service to the song. Then Corgan starts to sing and everything goes to hell. "I took my love, and I took it down," he begins, singing in that tiny sibilant whisper he always uses whenever he's trying to sound sincere. Like Stevie Nicks, Corgan takes us up the mountain so we can all turn around to see his "reflection in the snow-covered hills . . ." Unlike Nicks, Corgan has no clue as to what he's singing about. OK, he knows but he doesn't know, mostly because he's not a golden-maned California girl who was flat broke when she wrote the song.

Corgan moves on to the second stanza, somehow making himself sound less convincing than he was in the first one. He's still whispering but when he strains to hit the phrase, "Can I sail through changin' ocean tides?" you'd rather he just dove straight into the waves and be done with it. His voice is so nasal and pained, he sounds like he drop-kicked a Steinway. As he works his way into the bridge, his confidence seems to build in his voice and so do our migraines. "I've built my life around you," he whines, though the line's tender quality becomes just so much sandpaper. His interpretation of the key phrase of "Landslide," "I'm getting older, too," sounds really bad because I doubt he believes it, even if he does have to sing it twice.

By the time Corgan works his way back to the first stanza, he's found every way to distract us from the song's meaning by playing up his "alienation" and "disillusionment" with the world. He doesn't change the lyrics; he doesn't have to. Corgan could read *Thomas the Tank Engine* aloud and make it sound like some sulky teenager wrote it. Correction, he'd make it sound like he wrote it. When "Landslide" finally does end, you're digging yourself out from under the wave of suppressed bile that Corgan had on display.

Why It's Depressing

Do I hate the Smashing Pumpkins? No, but a little of their hyperkinetic alt-rock goes a long way with me. I've always found Corgan a little too serious for my tastes, anyway, especially when he declared he was ending Smashing Pumpkins because he felt they couldn't be part of an industry that was dominated by Britney Spears. Since when did she become so scary? It just comes down to the problem of a particular artist picking a song that is completely outside his or her genre. I know Pumpkin/Corgan fans will be disagreeing violently, but you know I'm right about this. "Landslide" was not meant to be sung by Billy Corgan.

Ditto the Dixie Chicks, who also covered the song. While they sing circles around Corgan, their version is too precious, with its bluegrass ornamentations and Grand Ole Opry harmonies. Again, I don't dislike the Dixie Chicks but their decision to cover "Landslide" turns the song into county fair muzak, and the contemplative words into defeatist mantras. Spread the word: Don't anybody cover "Landslide" ever again. You will just end up getting buried under it. In fact, I don't think Stevie Nicks should even sing it anymore. Let the young girl from 1975 have it forever, because it was hers to begin with.

Send in the Clowns

Performed by Judy Collins
Released 1975 (No. 6 in the UK, no. 19 in the US)
Also performed by Frank Sinatra, Barbra Streisand,
Acker Bilk, Betty Buckley, Roger Whittaker, Cleo Laine,
Shirley Horn, Grace Jones, et al
Words and music by Stephen Sondheim
(from *A Little Night Music*)

FIRST, a notice to all fledgling stage actresses: Never, ever, under any circumstances sing "Send in the Clowns" when auditioning for a musical. You'll be pegged as a neophyte, impaled on a skewer of queer vitriol, and tossed out on your waitress ass. This once-sublime show tune became a cyanide-gulping soporific long ago due to decades of other vocalists glomming onto it like flies on rancid mutton. "Send in the Clowns" is now the obligatory weeper that nightclub singers pull out of the trunk midway through the dinner show to try and make you sob into your veal. To really appreciate how cringe-inducing this Broadway standard has become, just know this: Even gays are sick of it.

"Send in the Clowns" originally appeared in the Stephen Sondheim musical *A Little Night Music*, which debuted in February 1973 at New York's Shubert Theater. Aging stage actress Glynis Johns playing the role of aging stage actress Desiree Armfeldt sat alone on the proscenium singing a cryptic lament to her doomed love for old flame Frederik Egerman. "Send in the clowns . . . ," she rasped out with resignation, making New York audiences weep openly while silently wondering what in the world she was talking about. The song serves as an enciphered denouement to Desiree Armfeldt's story line but after being lifted out of the Great White Way and thrown into the maw of pop music for so many years, "Send in the Clowns" has become a parody of itself, a dreary number that makes "Bridge over Troubled Water" sound like "Macarena."

The Song

Most people first became aware of "Send in the Clowns" via Judy Collins's 1975 lugubrious hit recording; listening to it, you'd swear she's standing in front of a firing squad. But to fully experience the throat-slitting misery of this song, one must hear it performed in that most horrifying of venues, a cabaret revue.

Imagine, if you will, a darkened lounge where you're sitting at a small table with your seventy-year-old aunt and uncle. You're still recovering from the last time they came into town to visit and took you to a community theater production of *You're a Good Man, Charlie Brown*. Tonight, they've dragged you to the Klip Klopp Supper Club for the 8 P.M. dinner show featuring "legendary song stylist" Mitzi Whosis. A spotlight is aimed at a red-draped stage the size of a billiards table where a creepy chanteuse who resembles Faye Dunaway after twenty skin grafts is sprawled on a Baldwin baby grand. For the past forty-five minutes, she's regaled you with mangled interpretations of Rodgers & Hart, Cole Porter, and, to show you that she's hip, selections from *The Lion King*. Now, she's staring off at some distant apparition only she can see, while piano music that sounds like Beethoven's Moonlight Sonata played sideways wafts quietly across the room. Closing her Blair Witch eyes, Mitzi begins: "Isn't it riiich? . . ." As she chews on the song's melody like a hyena feasting on a slow-moving yak, Mitzi tells you that she is on the ground watching someone in mid-air. OK, you ask, who? A window washer? A parachutist? The Silver

Surfer? Now she's unable to move as she watches the other person "tearing around." At the end of each stanza, she mournfully requests, "Send in the clowwwns . . ." You subtly motion to the waiter to send in the booze.

After a modulation into the bridge, Mitzi slithers off the piano to attack the song's thespian references with zombie relish. "Making my entrance again with my usual flaaair," she bellows, flailing her arms like Helen Keller fighting off an anaconda. But, alas, "no one is there," she mourns, dropping her voice to sibilant whisper. Your aunt's lower lip trembles violently, teardrops pooling around her half-eaten prime rib, as Mitzi tragically asks for someone to, damn it, "Send in the clowns . . ." "Right," you say to yourself, "and could one of the clowns bring along some matches and lighter fluid so I can set myself on fire?"

As Mitzi throws her waxen presence into the song's final verses, you gulp down your Jim Beam and water while silently praying her varicose veins don't explode. She's recalling how strange it is to lose her timing so late in her career. "Why?" you ask. "You've already lost your teeth." The spotlight grows smaller until it's focused only on her botox-ravaged face, as she groans out how there ought to be clowns on the stage with her by now, preferably ones who know CPR. "Maybe next yeaarrr," Mitzi concludes, then drops her head into a scoliosis crouch as your aunt and uncle applaud wildly before digging into the cheesecake. Mitzi gravely thanks the room then launches into a medley of songs by her "dear close friend" Carole Bayer Sager. Sighing, you smash your highball glass on the table and use the shards to cut into your jugular . . .

Why It's Depressing

"Send in the Clowns" suffers largely from Sondheim's obsessive wordsmith approach to lyric writing. He's known for going to great lengths to avoid being obvious, which is admirable, but his songs often work only within the context of the stage production in which they're featured. Plus, his lyrics sometimes sound like he shoved a thesaurus in a blender and set it on purée. Most listeners who bother to decipher "Send in the Clowns" assume it's about loss and regret. *Nein.* It's about self-pity, pure and simple, the poor-me whimperings of a withered prima donna who probably ate personal assistants for lunch. Besides, anybody who talks about entering a room with their usual flair needs to wear a sign around their neck that says "insufferable."

And that's basically what "Send in the Clowns" has become, an insufferably pretentious song that most singers handle the way Lizzie Borden handled an ax. I'm ashamed to say that I listened to a dozen different renditions of "Send in the Clowns" before the urge to climb the nearest bell tower with a high-powered rifle prevented me from venturing further. Of the numerous spirit-crushing versions I endured, the perverse standouts included Betty Buckley's try-and-top-me-bitch performance, Shirley Horn's jazz 'n' heroin crooning take, and Grace Jones's disco arrangement, which easily deserves a spot in the Bad Ideas Hall of Fame alongside New Coke and Windows Millennium.

Please keep it away from Celine Dion. I beg you . . .

I'm Telling a Story
Nobody Wants to
Hear

The River

Written and performed by Bruce Springsteen
Released 1980 (No. 35 in the UK)

MANY SONGWRITERS have a fixation with Americana, which shouldn't be confused with America, the rich nation that runs everything. America is a country, Americana is an existential concept filled with empty highways, waving fields of wheat, smoggy skylines of industrial decay, Graceland, wood-paneled taverns, and rustic characters who never have any money. America is wealthy and powerful, Americana is struggling and underdog. The Western world doesn't really like America very much but it loves Americana, which is the real reason the nations of Europe have never invaded the US, for fear of breaking Elvis figurines.

Bruce Springsteen is as Americana as it gets, no matter that he's rich enough to buy Madagascar, and nobody dons a wife-beater and poses unshaven for a photo better than he does. The Boss has been a working-class hero for some thirty years now, curious when you consider how lousy he makes blue-collar life sound. He's spun countless stories about simple folks with complex problems, all of them involving a car, a job, and a girl named Mary (most girls in Springsteen songs are named Mary). Downbeat themes have frequently been his template for songwriting and they work to varying degrees of success, "The River" not being one of them. The song is the title track from his 1980 double album, a work that addresses loss of innocence, heartbreak, disillusionment, and so on, themes that one must drone on about in order to be considered an "artist." I know

Boss fans are having a hemorrhage that I dare call him to task for writing this godawful depressing song but, frankly, I'd rather drag my scalp over a cheese grater than listen to it again.

The Song

"The River" begins with Bruce playing a twelve-string while mournfully wailing on a rack-mounted harmonica. I've never understood the harmonica rack. What mechanical De Sade invented that thing? ("Attention, musicians: I have a device that allows you to play the harmonica even shittier than you already do!") It's all very earnest and coffee house; you can practically see the "Open Mike Night" sign behind him. The song is Springsteen's 473rd first-person account about an unemployed dope with an unhappy wife (named Mary, of course). In "The River," we hear how a guy started dating Mary in high school, likely after going out with Mary Jane, Mary Ann, and Mary Lou. As The E-Street Band kicks in at the chorus, the relevance of the river is introduced. In their free time, he and Mary liked to go "down to the river" where they dived in, swam, frolicked, laughed, had sex, got pregnant, and ruined their lives. With Mary preggers, the guy brings her over to the courthouse to get married so he can make an honest woman out of her. For his nineteenth birthday, he sadly tells us how he received "a union card and a wedding coat." The scenario is revealing itself to be rather dreary, but then again, this is what he's supposed to do. See, where he lives, they bring you up ". . . to do like your daddy done." If this is true, then Asbury Park, New Jersey, has got a lot of explaining to do. The chorus returns again, bringing the hapless young newlyweds back to the river where all their troubles started. This time, all the splashing in the water isn't nearly as much fun because Mary doesn't look as hot in her swimsuit as she did before.

So now what? What does the young Jersey misfit with no

education and a new wife and baby do in this idyllic situation? Naturally, he's going to get stuck in a crappy job because no protagonist in a Springsteen song ever works anywhere cool. In "The River," he starts a contruction job for the Johnstown Company, but soon gets laid off because he's in a Springsteen song. So now things that were so important before (like not being married) are gone forever and he's stuck at home on a cold Asbury Park morning with a screaming baby and a grouchy wife who cannot fathom why she agreed to let him nail her out on the banks of that stupid river a year earlier.

A musical bridge lets him reminisce about those swell times back at the river, when he and (sigh) Mary used to lie out by the reservoir where he could check out her pre-motherhood figure. But now the river's dry and he wonders "is a dream a lie if it don't come true." Keep in mind this guy is, like, twenty now yet he's feeling nostalgic for fourteen months earlier, a young and free time when . . . he wasn't married with a kid.

Why It's Depressing

Springsteen has written far better blue-collar anthems than "The River" over the years so why critics and fans hold this boring, depressing song in such high regard is beyond me. It's nothing more than the pathetic grumbling of a guy wearing a Cat Diesel baseball cap, denim workshirt, and wispy mustache who you had the misfortune of sitting next to at the bar. He peaked when he was seventeen and it's been all downhill since, something he'll be more than happy to tell you about since you're on the adjacent stool. I know the chimp-simple lyrics are intentionally written that way to give a voice to a guy with limited education but are we really that interested? Just once I'd love to hear Bruce sing about somebody getting plastered on Cristal and driving a Bentley into a swimming pool.

"The River" goes to a lot of trouble to tell us about two of the most uninteresting people to ever fail the rabbit test and end up getting hitched at city hall while simultaneously showing how much it bites to be a member of the working class. It is not a deep, profound, and touching song by any means, nor is it even necessary. Many of us went to school with kids like the hapless couple in Springsteen's song and we kept them at a guarded distance back then. "The River," on the other hand, brings their dreary life story into our car radio time and again, so no matter how much you yell at the receiver, you're still going to have to hear it.

Let's face it, why would anybody want to star in a Springsteen song? You'll just end up unemployed with a resentful wife (named Mary), bratty kids, and a broken-down car while spending every waking day wondering how your life got so screwed up. Evidently, nobody in Springsteen's blue-collar hell ever gets promoted to manager or is able to afford a Lexus. They instead exist in a proletarian hell where mortgages are foreclosed, transmissions leak, and wives have a "headache" every night.

It's enough to make you want to go to college. If Bruce will let you.

The Freshmen

Performed by the Verve Pipe
Released 1997 (No. 1 in the US)
Written by Brian Vander Ark

NOT TO BE confused with the English group the Verve, the American grunge-lite band the Verve Pipe came out of the upper Midwest (Michigan specifically) in the 1990s, playing alt-rock music while waiting for Britney and *NSYNC to come along and ruin everything. They scored a hit single in 1997 with their memorably depressing song "The Freshmen," which recounts the misery of two young men dealing with the suicide of a girl they both dated and dumped while in college. Its lyrical hook of "I can't be held responsible . . ." struck a chord with millions of teenagers since it's the very same line they utter anytime they put a scratch on Dad's car.

The Verve Pipe are fronted by lead vocalist Brian Vander Ark, a very good songwriter who unfortunately has the ability to sound exactly (and I mean exactly) like Kurt Cobain whenever he belts, albeit with better diction. It's not anything intentional, that's just the way he sings. He's undoubtedly been chided for it, which is too bad as both his group and Nirvana were formed thousands of miles apart from each other around the same time. Melancholy and tragic, "The Freshmen" stood apart from the mumbling angst of the fading Seattle music scene if only because you could clearly understand the words. The song's lo-fi sincerity (there's literally no reverb on the vocals), however, made critics cluck their tongues, preferring their musical anxieties to be obscure and indecipherable.

The Song

"The Freshmen" features some fine musical dynamics, with the music slowly building throughout while a snare drum lays down an insistent military-like cadence. The song opens with a striking electric guitar figure, which immediately conjures up images of boarding school, empty campus grounds, and any scene from *Dawson's Creek* where James Van Der Beek gazes longingly at a departing Katie Holmes. "When I was young I knew everything," Vander Ark begins, singing in such a direct, honest way that we can forgive him for opening with such a tired line. It's somebody's wedding day and the first-person narrator has just learned the girl he dated back in college has killed herself. Naturally, this puts a damper on the day's nuptials and he's wracked with guilt, "sobbing, with my head on the floor."

Vander Ark is creating a scene out of one of those self-absorbed indie films that Miramax used to release back in the 1990s when they were still under the illusion anybody wanted to see them. Two groomsmen in their twenties wearing tuxedoes are seated in the back room of a church, their bow ties undone, looking lost to the world as they absorb the traumatic news they've heard. Both of them have ducked out of the wedding they were supposed to turn up for, forcing the ceremony to proceed without them. They're conversing about the girl because they share a history with her. One of them finally utters the song's signature lyric, "I can't be held responsible . . . ," which naturally makes us wonder, hmm, why would you be? It soon becomes apparent that both of them slept with her, only to dump her later. The narrator cannot fathom why either of them ever thought they were mature adults at the time. Hell, they aren't even that now. Back then, "we were merely freshmen."

Vander Ark continues, saying how his best friend took off for a spell in order to forget the girl. Unfortunately, this second act of rejection compels her to down a bottle of Valium, not quite the reaction anyone was expecting. "Now he's guilt-ridden, sobbing, with his head on the floor." This particular line makes three appearances in the song and you wonder if these two are mourning the girl's passing or just anxious for someone to let them off the hook. Though it's never revealed how much time has passed since either of them last saw her, it would seem fairly recent.

"We've tried to wash our hands of all this," Vander Ark rasps, his voice cracking into Cobain territory. Both guys admit that neither of them ever bothered to have a serious relationship. Now they're both sobbing . . .

The song is filled with nervous MIDI string fills, which lend an effective texture while the guitars go from clean to dirty so subtly, you don't notice it until they're at full grind. After Vander Ark's vocals work their way up to maximum shred, he drops them down to their original plaintive state. He repeats, "We were merely freshmen . . ."

Why It's Depressing

For a song that tackles such a grim subject, "The Freshmen" has far more shelf life than its competitors. It's expertly performed and produced, and I've no doubt couples watching the Verve Pipe perform it live lay their heads on each other's shoulders while silently mouthing along with the words. The song's success, however, tossed the Verve Pipe into the dreaded one-hit-wonder category, all the more unfortunate as I've found "The Freshmen" to be atypical of the group's otherwise hard-rocking style.

While I admit it's an effective song, "The Freshmen" bums me out no end. Hearing about a college girl gulping down a bottle of sleeping pills from the two guilt-ravaged heels who abandoned her is something I need experience only once. There's just a tad too much guilt-ridden sobbing in "The Freshmen" for my taste, though I give the Verve Pipe credit for tackling a serious subject without having it blow up in their faces. In these cynical times, it's not easy to write a hit song filled with so much pathos and they were able to pull it off successfully enough to saddle themselves with it for a long time. It's a given that "The Freshmen" is a required addition to the Verve Pipe playlist and as long as the group is intact, they'll have to revisit a young girl's suicide over and over again. So many music artists come to resent the one big song that made them famous and when it's a depressing one like "The Freshmen," it becomes the world's biggest anchor around their collective necks.

Comfortably Numb

Performed by Pink Floyd
Released 1980
Written by Roger Waters and David Gilmour

THE CREAKY rock "concept" album is one musical relic that must never be resurrected. What's the point? Concept albums are all about being heavy-handed and nothing had weightier mitts than Pink Floyd's 1979 *The Wall*. It was that rare double album people owned out of obligation. Nobody ever listened to the entire thing in one sitting unless they owned a bong the size of a mop; most instead chose to "experience" it one side at a time. It was only many years later, while deep into marriages and mortgages, that a generation of former Floydheads looked back on their *Wall* experiences and confessed, "Christ, that album was really a downer—at least what I heard of it."

Indeed. So the obvious question is how do you select a *Wall* track as being the most depressing when the entire album isn't exactly a chucklefest? Simple. Try to think which song off *The Wall* still casts a pall of utter gloom over you no matter how many times vintage rock stations spin it in between Lynyrd Skynyrd and Bad Company? That's right, "Comfortably Numb."

The Song

Since "Comfortably Numb" is a part of *The Wall*'s narrative, uninitiated readers should first know the entire album's storyline from beginning to end. Ready? Here goes. There's this rock star named Pink. And a big wall. OK, you're set.

At this point in *The Wall* saga, Pink is now famous and a complete emotional wreck. (Boo friggin' hoo.) He's been sent to undergo sinister mental manipulations by some Peter Lorre-type quack whose part is sung by bassist Roger Waters. As anyone familiar with Pink Floyd's history knows, Waters was the curmudgeon of the group, a dour, humorless songwriter whose dour, humorless voice was usurped by guitarist David Gilmour's pleasing tenor. "Comfortably Numb" begins with Waters croaking out the verse part as he examines Pink while backed by a slow ethereal crawl of minor chord guitars and analog effects. "Hello," he intones, "is there anybody in there?" He tells Pink that he needs some information first. The music modulates to the relative major in the bridge as a zonked Pink wordlessly responds through Gilmour's plaintive voice how "your lips move but I can't hear what you're saying." He relates how, as a child, he once had a fever that left his head feeling like a balloon. Now the pressures of fame, riches, groupie sex, or whatever have left him feeling just like that again but, hey, we just wouldn't understand. Instead, Pink has become "comfortably numb . . ."

A numb rock star? Say it ain't so. What else to do but ply the gaunt twit with lots of inoculations? "You'll feel a little pin prick," Waters's doctor sings cynically, rubbing his palms together greedily as Pink is chemically slapped awake. Record company henchmen grab Pink by his skinny arms and drag him to the stage, throwing him out to the heartless crowd, etcetera, etcetera. Pink reminisces one last time about being a child, catching a glimpse of "distant ships, smoke on the horizon." But they disappeared and now he's grown and the "dream is gone." (What dream, to work for a cruise line?) The song ends with a piledriver guitar solo from Gilmour (a great one, to be sure) before fading into the next chapter of Pink's sorry tale.

Why It's Depressing

"Comfortably Numb" may be the most appropriately titled song ever written. If there ever was a recording that could substitute for Demerol, this is the one. Never a single, "Comfortably Numb" still gets a lot of airplay on rock stations, so you may run the risk of being lulled off the highway into a ditch should it suddenly emanate from your car radio. This song just misses out on being a legitimately sad one, if only because Roger Waters sings on it. Borderline genius as he is, Waters has never been much of a vocalist. To many, he has two approaches to singing: grumble during the slow songs; rant during the fast ones. When he's really wound up, he sounds like he's channeling every fanatic to show up at Speakers' Corner in London's Hyde Park armed with a soapbox and a conspiracy theory. Granted, Waters is very low-key and unctuous as the evil medico who jabs needles into Pink to get him prepped for the 9 P.M. show at Hammersmith Odeon, but a purring Roger Waters is still scarier than a bellowing David Gilmour. Waters's solo albums are undoubtedly filled with songs that are real mindfuckers, but they don't count. The only people who buy them want to get depressed.

The other issue with "Comfortably Numb" is how difficult it is to empathize with the wounded Pink. The tortured rock star bit went south years ago after the music-buying public saw the aerial photos of Axl Rose's mansion. "Comfortably Numb" should really be called "Comfortably Rich."

The Wreck of the Edmund Fitzgerald

Performed by Gordon Lightfoot
Released 1976 (No. 40 in the UK, no. 2 in the US)
Words and Music by Gordon Lightfoot

WHILE HUNDREDS of themes have been addressed in contemporary pop songs, I can safely say that shipwrecks rank near the bottom of the list. Other than the *Titanic*, who really remembers any great sea tragedies that warranted a song? The *Lusitania*? The *Andrea Doria*? That's why the American record industry was so taken aback when Canadian folk singer Gordon Lightfoot's long moody ballad "The Wreck of the Edmund Fitzgerald" sailed its way (sorry) to number two in the US in 1976. The song had everything that you don't find in a hit single, namely a glacial tempo, 14,000 words, and no love story. Lightfoot had been a mainstay of Canadian music for years and had scored a number-one hit in 1974 with his laid-back yet intense song "Sundown." He charted two more singles, then came to the table with the epic "Edmund Fitzgerald," a six-minute-long song that he crammed onto a 45-rpm record. Mystified, executives at his record company scratched their heads and asked the question that was on everyone's minds: What the hell is the *Edmund Fitzgerald*?

The SS *Edmund Fitzgerald* was a 729-foot freighter that plied the Great Lakes for seventeen years, hauling cargo just as hundreds of other ships did. On November 10, 1975, the *Edmund Fitzgerald* left Superior, Wisconsin, and was on its way to Detroit when it ran into a terrible storm. The captain steered toward the Canadian port city of Whitefish Bay in Ontario province, but could not outrun the tempest. The ship broke apart and sank to the bottom of Lake Superior, taking twenty-nine crewmen and 26,000 tons of iron ore pellets with it. Some time later, a memorial service was held at a cathedral in Detroit where the church bell was rung twenty-nine times in remembrance of the perished seamen.

Having said all this, I've just discovered that I've screwed myself. Everything that I recounted about the *Edmund Fitzgerald* is exactly the same tale that Lightfoot sings about in his song (he changes one detail for the sake of a rhyme, but whatever . . .). Therefore, analyzing it means you, the reader, will have to endure hearing this sad story all over again. (This is a hint as to why I consider this song so depressing.)

The Song

To his credit, Lightfoot begins "Edmund Fitzgerald" in a manner not usually found in a folk song: channeling Pink Floyd. The song opens with a mournful electric guitar hook that is so *Dark Side of the Moon*, I'm surprised Dave Gilmour never asked for royalties. While he insistently strums his acoustic, Lightfoot introduces us to the legend of Lake Superior, this being that she "never gives up her dead," especially in November when the weather gets cold and nasty. He then details the *Edmund Fitzgerald*'s cargo capacity while ominously describing the ship and its personnel as "a bone to be chewed." For years, I found this metaphor odd until I realized that "chew" rhymes with "crew." Lightfoot tries to show off his acumen regarding specific details, saying how they concluded "some terms with a couple of steel firms" before setting sail, "fully loaded for Cleveland." This by the way is wrong, as the ship was destined for Detroit but, hey, how many words rhyme with "Detroit"?

After some drums come in and the Floydian guitar plays its break (the same one, note for note), the *Edmund Fitzgerald* gets under way. Lightfoot brings us onboard the freighter, describing in detail the waves breaking over the rails, the howling wind, the freezing rain, the rough conditions. "Fellas, it's too rough to feed ya," he has the cook tell the crew. Once a hatchway gives way and the ship begins taking on water, that's the beginning of the end. Lightfoot has the ship turning toward Whitefish Bay while its captain radios for help (any of this sound familiar?), but it's all for naught. When its "lights went out of sight, came the wreck of the *Edmund Fitzgerald* . . ."

Afterward, the searchers find no survivors and the freighter lies undisturbed at the bottom of 550 feet of water. Lightfoot doesn't elect to end the tale here, though, but instead goes overboard (sorry again) by working all five Great Lakes into the sixth stanza, telling how "Lake Huron rolls, Superior sings" and "Lake Michigan streams like a young man's dreams . . ." Lake Ontario? She just takes what "Lake Erie can send her." I've no idea what compelled Lightfoot to feature the names of all the Great Lakes other than to show he's a whiz at geography.

The memorial service in Detroit concludes the song, where we learn of the bell that rang twenty-nine times. We've also learned that the music has been repeating itself over and over without so much as a bridge, chorus, or blues jam. In fact, what you hear during the intro is what you get for the entire song. The Floydian slip guitar riff that opened the song closes it, too, the guy having practiced it so much we can assume he probably has it down cold by now.

Why It's Depressing

This song has particular meaning to me because I have some proximity to the events depicted in "Wreck of the Edmund Fitzgerald," being that I'm from Wisconsin. My connection to the freighter ends there, as it does with most Wisconsinites. The tragedy has never really caught on as part of state lore and was largely forgotten months after it happened. Yet this didn't stop local stations from playing "Wreck of the Edmund Fitzgerald" every ten minutes back in 1976 and, consequently, we were bombarded with this rhyme-infested sea shanty during an entire summer of lawnmowing and touch football. You could not go anywhere without hearing about the cook, the captain, the crew, and ye olde "gales of November" that chewed them all up like a bone. Lightfoot is quite thorough in telling the story; the lyrics read like a newspaper article—and therein lies the problem. Newspapers are read once then used to wrap fish, so hearing the recounting of a ship taking the plunge with twenty-nine people aboard gets increasingly difficult to take in ongoing doses. As soon as you hear Lightfoot's twelve-string and that Floydian guitar hook, your mind immediately races ahead and starts sinking the freighter before he even starts singing. It's like watching the same downbeat movie with a sad ending twenty times in a row. Eventually, your catharsis turns to contempt and you just wish he'd jump ahead to the cathedral for all the ceremony.

Maggie's Dream

Performed by Don Williams
Released 1984 (No. 11 on the Country charts in the US)
Words and Music by Dave Loggins and Lisa Silver

COUNTRY MUSIC fans have probably noticed a dearth of country song titles in this book. "Where's 'The Long Black Veil'? Where's 'He Stopped Lovin' Her Today'? Where's Tammy Wynette?" Having once been a disc jockey at a country music station in Texas (true), I had my fill of songs about drinkin', lyin', and cheatin'. I never considered them as anything other than pitchfork morality tales. George Jones was more depressing to look at than to hear sing, and the Judds seemed harmless enough. Naturally, I found some country songs aggravating, especially the Nashville-cum-Vegas releases; hearing 1980s-era Barbara Mandrell and Kenny Rogers reminds me more of slot machines than pickup trucks. Otherwise, the music didn't have much of an effect on me. I showed up on time, spun the requested tunes, and learned to tolerate the steel guitar.

Then, one day, "Maggie's Dream" showed up.

This hemlock-swilling weeper still holds a dark and special place in my life for being, if I may use the vernacular, the firs' country music song tha' made me wanna throw mah-self inna a vat o' steamin' possum shee-it. Or at least shove steak knives into my ears. Lethargic and miserable, "Maggie's Dream" tells the tale of a lonely waitress who's spent thirty years working at a diner outside Asheville, North Carolina (spelled "Ashville" in the lyrics fer some dad-gum reason). She's never married, never left Asheville, and is destined to die alone. Yee-hah!!

The song was released in 1984 by veteran Nashville singer Don Williams, known to rock audiences for writing the minor Eric Clapton hit "Tulsa Time." A large man, Williams has long been dubbed the "Gentle Giant" for his easygoing demeanor and laid-back approach to music. I'm sure he's a great guy and I've always liked "Tulsa Time," but God forbid he ever gets hold of a vein-drainer like "Maggie's Dream" again. Although he didn't write it, he skillfully wrings out a pathetic tale of rural bleakness that would compel a teetotaller to guzzle a tanker's worth of Jack Daniel's.

The Song

"Maggie's up each morning at 4 A.M.," Williams begins in his velvety baritone over an easy-listening Nashville track of acoustic guitar and cloying electric piano. He gets her to the truckstop diner Café Carolina at 5 A.M. prompt. Maggie, we learn, is diligent, reliable, and punctual. She's also a porker. We're never told this but, hey: waitress, truckstop, platters of fried food? You do the math. Soon her trucker friends will be a-rollin' in, wavin' their hellos to Maggie as they settle up to the counter wearing their Mack caps. They all like her, all say she's swell, all think she's a chunker. Williams gives us Maggie's unremarkable history, specifically that she's worked at the café most all her life, "thirty years of coffee cups and sore feet," while pointing out how she's never been outside of Asheville. Worse yet, Maggie's getting close to fifty.

It's during the song's depressing chorus that we find out the real problem. "Maggie's never had a love," Williams sings, the reason being she's never had the time to allow a man into her life. So, then, what is Maggie's dream? "To find a husband and be a wife." That's it. Maggie wants to be married. And she's been waiting thirty years for it to happen.

I need to interrupt here. This chorus has always stuck in my craw if only because Maggie claims she's never had the time to find a man to be with. Never had the time? I've eaten at plenty of truckstops and I can tell you that time comes to a screeching halt in most of them. They're all Formica, fried eggs, and flat inertia. There ain't nothin' so whirlwind about the Café Carolina that she couldn't have found the time. It's not like she's working the floor at the Stock Exchange.

Williams continues, telling us how Maggie knows most of her truckers by name, along with their usual orders and whatever stories they have to tell. For three decades, she's chatted with them, all the while hoping in vain that one of them will take an interest in her. Instead, they leave her with "the dishes, dreams, and quarters."

After a repeat of the chorus, Williams goes into a bridge in which he goes all out to break our spirits. With the truckers out on the road, business slows down in the afternoon at the Café Carolina. This is when poor lonely Maggie goes to the jukebox and "plays the saddest tunes" (including this one, probably). Finally, she goes to the window, "stares out at the highway and wonders where it goes." She reminds herself how she has nobody waiting for her at home. Meanwhile, it's almost closing time . . .

Why It's Depressing

Since this song was on the playlist at the station where I worked, I had to endure Maggie's sad, sad life for I don't know how long. I imagined her ignominious upbringing, including her graduating high school 143rd in her class, an unrequited crush on the boy who worked at the feed store, and starting at the Café Carolina part-time as a waitress, a job she assumed would be temporary. Thirty years later, she's still there, alone, frozen, and big as Mrs. Jumbo.

Williams abandons fattie Maggie at the truckstop but, let's face it, she could turn this around. Remember, Maggie works at a business whose clientele are 90 percent male. There's no reason why she couldn't lay off the pork chops for a while, take some aerobics classes (do they have those in North Carolina?), and then stroll into the truckstop with her newly svelte figure and give a wink and a smile to a couple of guys. In fact, I want Maggie to do this just so I can erase Williams's song about her from my long-term memory. I'm incapable of dealing with any story about a trapped desperate middle-aged waitress who's spent thirty years wondering why no one will love her. Yee-hah!!

People Who Died

Performed by the Jim Carroll Band
Released 1981 (No. 51 in the US)
Written by Jim Carroll

MORE THAN a few punk songs were suggested for inclusion in this book. I gave them a listen but found them all to be lacking in the depressing department. Too much punk music sounds to me like screaming winos crammed inside a runaway shopping cart; hardly any of it makes me despondent. Jittery, yes; twitchy, yes; compelled to wear a mohawk, sure; but not despondent. Then I recalled a punk song from long ago that I had the unusual experience of actually hearing on the radio. It featured one of the more unusual choruses I'd ever heard: "Those are people who died! Died! Those are people who died! Died . . ." I unearthed it, took it for a spin, and found myself wanting to snap ten-penny nails in half with my teeth. As depressing punk songs go, I challenge anyone to top "People Who Died."

This notorious death anthem comes courtesy of New York–based poet/writer/singer/former junkie Jim Carroll, best known for his memoir *The Basketball Diaries*, which was made into a 1995 feature film starring a pre-*Titanic* Leo DiCaprio. Never remotely a hit, "People Who Died" has become a cult favorite among humorless hipsters who sigh with envy every time they hear about somebody who OD'd on the subway.

Born in 1950, Jim Carroll grew up in New York City and was a stand-out basketball player at his high school. He was also a heroin addict, which pretty much screwed up his game but prepped him for his future career as a tortured artist that critics jizz themselves over. He published *The Basketball Diaries* in 1970, then formed a rock band a few years later during the advent of New York's punk rock scene. Musically, the Jim Carroll Band sounded like Iggy and the Stooges except with a different fuck-up leading them. He released his debut album, *Catholic Boy*, in 1980, featuring "People Who Died," a thrashing song where Carroll frantically spits out the names and cause of death of various acquaintances in his social circle. Some people familiar with the song consider it a perverse novelty number from a punk band trying to audition for Dr. Demento. Me, I just think it's messed up. Still, "People Who Died" remains a stand-out song of the punk genre because every word of it, allegedly, is true.

The Song

"Edmund Fitzgerald" aside, all the depressing songs that address death in this book feature only one victim, with Bloodrock's "DOA" serving up two. Now consider the body count in "People Who Died": thirteen, with three of them named Bobby. That's a baker's dozen of Jim Carroll's friends ". . . who died! Died!" And, oh, how they died, died: drug overdoses, stepping in front of subway trains, throat slitting, hanging, falling from roofs, jumping from roofs, being thrown from roofs, and so on. I'm not sure what the odds are that one person would know this many dead individuals other than if they all shared the same smack dealer.

The music on "People Who Died" is vintage punk, with concussion-infused drums and speedball guitars thrashing out an amped-up Chuck Berry riff (besides the Stooges, I suspect Carroll listened closely to X). Carroll's spitfire vocals make you realize this song is far from the usual safety pin stuff. "Teddy sniffing glue, he was twelve years old!" he says/sings. "Fell from the roof on east two-nine . . . !" Any follow-up reflection? No, Carroll is already on to his next statistic, that being an eleven-year-old girl named Cathy who died by ingesting twenty-six reds and washing them down with a bottle of wine. Then Bobby number one got leukemia when he was fourteen, looking like sixty-five by the time he died . . . It takes Carroll under fifteen seconds to recount all of these awful 'tween deaths, which just shows you how fast he's rapping and how bizarre his childhood was. The song's twisted chorus is what fans loved: "Those are people who died! Died . . . !" he chants with soccer hooligan zeal.

So who else gets offed in this song? Well, there's G-berg and Georgie (hepatitis), Sly (Vietnam) and Bobby number two who, Carroll shrieks, "OD'd on Drano on the night that he was wed!" Assuming this is true, and I've no doubt it is, just how bad can things be that you'd guzzle drain cleaner on your wedding night? More importantly, the question begs, who were these people? I think it's at this point I want to ask Jim Carroll, "Did you ever hang out with anybody, y'know, normal?"

After a frenetic (and unnecessary) guitar break, Carroll resumes his obituary column. Mary throws herself off a building, Bobby number three hangs himself, Judy takes a powder by jumping in front of a subway train, Eddie gets his throat cut. At the end of each repeat of the yelping chorus, the same line: "They were all my friends, and they died!!" When Carroll adds more murders to his death list, you seriously wonder what the hell's going on. Herbie, he tells us, pushed his friend Tony off a roof (the third building-related death in this song) just for the hell of it, while somebody named Brian got whacked for snitching on some bikers. By this time, you're completely drained and start wishing for some sunshine and roses to appear and light up Carroll's life. Instead, he makes the odd choice of starting the song over again. He sings about twelve-year-old Teddy sniffing glue for a second time, taking us all the way through Eddie's demise, thereby stretching the song to a torturous five minutes, while forcing the guitarist's hand to start bleeding. Once again: "They were all my friends, and they died!"

Why It's Depressing

If it weren't for the pounding music and lack of sentiment, this song might've been a Perfect Storm. The contrast of classic punk thrashing with Carroll's Grim Reaper lyrics is what makes "People Who Died" so appealing to its fans, who clearly relish that every word of it is true. As death songs go, this one is by and large the most banal. Carroll offers no comment or moralizing about his friends' untimely deaths, just that "I miss 'em. They died." Had Carroll gotten all preachy and cautionary, he could've created a Perfect Storm, but he chose to stick to the facts.

For me, what makes "People Who Died" so relentlessly depressing is that Jim Carroll seemingly never knew anybody who passed away in their sleep from old age. Right off the bat, three kids who were fourteen and under are dead, and it just gets worse. Then again, living to a ripe old age would be a probable sign of a stable life, something that most artists disdain and no critic wants to hear about. Plus, not too many words rhyme with "natural causes."

Strange Fruit

Performed by Billie Holiday
Released 1939 (No. 16 in the US)
Arranged by Danny Mendelsohn
Based on the poem by "Lewis Allan" (Abel Meeropol)

ALTHOUGH she is today considered one of music's greatest vocalists, Billie Holiday didn't sell nearly as many records as the Lennon Sisters and Frank Sinatra did during her heyday and she's more recognized now for being on postage stamps than for her music. Even some music critics get Billie Holiday wrong, referring to her as a blues singer. (She wasn't; Holiday recorded only one real blues song throughout her entire career.) The stereotypical image of Billie is of a damaged woman standing alone on a dark stage, a pin spot illuminating her mournful face as she sings a mournful torch song about a man who done her wrong. This is about 38 percent accurate, 40 percent if you stick a gardenia in her hair.

In truth, Billie's legacy was built on hip yet unpretentious renditions of popular songs. Many of them were unremarkable by themselves, yet she transformed them into swinging works of art. Jazz historian James Lincoln Collier described Holiday best, saying in effect that she knew a song's value instinctively in her gut and was able to strip it down to its bare bones and perform it in the proper context—in other words, she knew not to oversell a weak tune. As far as songs go, she recorded as many up-tempo swingers as she did moody numbers, her best work done with small combos featuring tenor saxophonist Lester Young. So why her tortured reputation? Granted, she did have drug problems and her choices in men were not the wisest. But it's also partly to do with her most famous song, the notorious "Strange Fruit."

For those unfamiliar with it, "Strange Fruit" is a song about lynching and quite graphic, too, even by today's standards. Contrary to popular belief, "Strange Fruit" was not written by Holiday or by any African-American (its lyrics are often erroneously attributed to the poet Langston Hughes). The song was actually composed by a white Jewish socialist named Abel Meeropol, who wrote under the pen name Lewis Allan. It began life as a poem until Meeropol, an amateur musician, set his verses to agitprop-style music. As the story goes, Meeropol sat down at a piano and performed "Strange Fruit" for Holiday who, strangely enough, had no idea what he was singing about. Unimpressed, she passed on the song until a friend of hers persuaded her to give it a shot. Her accompanist, Sonny White, "jazzed" up the song's plodding music by adding thick dissonant minor chords and she began performing "Strange Fruit" during her shows.

Within weeks, "Strange Fruit" created a stir around New York City. To meet audience expectations, Billie began stretching out the song while performing, making it longer and more pretentious. No doubt tipsy patrons inside a smoky nightclub found this mesmerizing but if you had a clear head and looked past the nicotine clouds, you could see it was mostly theater. She eventually recorded "Strange Fruit" and it became a Top 20 hit in the US. Though it still registers with people today, "Strange Fruit" is a horribly depressing song and many jazz purists dislike that she ever recorded it because it's not the Billie Holiday they know.

The Song

"Strange Fruit" opens with a small ensemble of bluesy trumpets, saxes, piano, and rhythm section playing an "overture" to set the mood. Dark and ominous, it hardly qualifies as great jazz, sounding more like music you'd hear while watching a private eye strolling on a rainy night wearing a trenchcoat. The horns drop out and the piano plays a moody theme (detective lights cigarette . . .) for a solid minute (detective adjusts fedora . . .). Overly long, this intro was added merely to pad out the song so record buyers wouldn't feel cheated (it would've lasted less than two minutes without it). Billie's husky voice finally appears, singing about how "Southern trees bear strange fruit," describing the blood on their leaves and roots. The fruit in question is "black bodies swinging in the Southern breeze."

Audiences of the time picked up right away on what she was singing about and reactions were understandably mixed. Some customers stormed out in disgust as she performed it. Others found the song powerful and kept requesting it. The angry lyrics depict a scene filled with "bulging eyes" and "twisted mouth" while the magnolia-scented air is overcome with the stench of "burning flesh." Billie delivers all these pulpy images in a mournful voice as muted trumpets hover around her.

The song's final stanza has Billie singing how crows will ravage this strange fruit while it swings in the wind and rain. Here is fruit, she concludes, "for the sun to rot." It is a "strange and bitter crop." Strange and bitter indeed. And brief, mercifully brief.

Why It's Depressing

Debates among jazz aficionados over "Strange Fruit" still rage at times, usually over the issue of covering it. Many Billie Holiday acolytes feel it's her song and no one else should sing it. Some jazz vocalists from Carmen MacRae to Nina Simone, Dee Dee Bridgewater to Cassandra Wilson have recorded versions of "Strange Fruit," all of them respectful and dreary. It's not their fault, because "Strange Fruit" is a dreary song

(John Martyn's version, no jazz singer he, is dreadful). There's really no way to interpret "Strange Fruit" except as a grim ballad; any other way would be perverse. The grotesque lyrics are Southern gothic by way of Minsky's and, while no doubt earnest, do more to exploit the repulsive tragedy of lynching than condemn it. The melody that Holiday pulled like gum on a hot sidewalk is at best adequate and resembles a weak variation of the standard "Angel Eyes."

"Strange Fruit" would follow Holiday throughout her career until her death in 1957 at the age of forty-two. Since then, the song has remained a hot button topic in the jazz world. As stated earlier, there were many people who disliked "Strange Fruit" (including the legendary John Hammond, who discovered Billie) because they felt it overshadowed her work as a superb interpreter of popular song while exaggerating her persona as a wounded torch singer with a shattered heart and smeared mascara. Even today, it's not unusual for jazz singers to have crises of conscience when faced with the option of performing the song, feeling they're not worthy enough to sing it. The truth is it's more like the other way around.

DOA

Performed by Bloodrock
Released 1971 (No. 36 in the US)
Written by Jim Rutledge, Rick Cobb, Ed Grundy, Steve Hill,
Lee Pickens, and Nick Taylor

ABANDON all hope, ye who enter here. That's all I can say about "DOA," an ode to the ephemeral joy that comes with winding up on a coroner's slab. Death metal fans can rave about Rob Zombie all they want, but this horror show of a tune, sung from the point of view of a bloody corpse, kicks necrophilia ass over anything he's ever conceived. The fact that it was released as a single, for God's sake, only enhances its perverse stature in the Depressing Song Hall of Fame.

"DOA" is the work of Bloodrock, a blues-rock group from Texas whose ignominious career rivals Badfinger's minus the suicides. A poor man's Grand Funk Railroad, they frequently toured as the opening act for the critically lambasted power trio while releasing half a dozen albums for Capital Records (if any reader actually owns one, please call me so I can ask you why). Today, Bloodrock is basically forgotten and they would otherwise rest in obscurity if it weren't for this damned song.

The Song

"DOA" begins with an ominous Hammond organ playing a see-sawing figure that mimics a European ambulance siren (*nee-nuu nee-nuu . . .*) before we hear from the song's narrator, a broken and mangled corpse who lies in a morgue staring at the ceiling. In true Wes Craven fashion, said corpse starts describing everything around him in grisly detail: the blood running down his arms, the searing pain in his back, the white sheet across his chest. Worse still, his willowy blonde girlfriend lies dead on the slab next to him. "The girl I knew has such a distant stare," the singer opines wretchedly. He then breaks into an eerie chorus that explains how he met his demise in a plane crash: "I remember we were flying along and hit something in the airrrr . . ."

What brought down his plane the narrator never explains; he may have crashed into a barn while crop dusting for all we know. Rest assured, though, that the whole thing was pretty gruesome as American emergency sirens come screaming into the background while the organ continues its doom-laden Eurocentric ambulance vamp (it seems this aviation tragedy spread across two continents). As the narrator lies there, a morgue attendant appears and looks down at him, clucking his tongue, before whispering "there's no chance for me."

Umm, what?

Not to be a stickler about morgue etiquette, but what kind of forensic attendant stands over a busted-up corpse and declares there's no chance left for him? Did the discovery of the *Titanic* prompt anyone to say, "Hey, you think this thing will ever float again?" I'm no pathologist but if the medical authorities deem it necessary to drop a patient off at the morgue, the odds are he or she is impending worm food. The lyric is meant, of course, to underscore the narrator's terminal condition, but we're pretty clear on that issue after the first line of the song, "laying here staring at the ceiling . . ." Translation: Look at me, I'm dead.

The narrator of "DOA" is so vivid in describing his surroundings I can only assume that he's having one of those out-of-body experiences that afflicted Patrick Swayze in the movie *Ghost* twenty years later. As the song lumbers on, the narrator feels his life slipping away as the pain "flows out with my blood." He stridently cries to God to teach him how to die, an odd request considering he's been pretty thorough at describing death for the past four minutes. "DOA" ends with a cacophony of sirens fading off in the distance, leaving the listener to gaze slack-jawed at the floor and ask the burning question, "OK, what was that all about?"

Why It's Depressing

Isn't it obvious? Everything about "DOA" is depressing, from its ubiquitous dirge organ (*nee-nuu nee-nuu . . .*) and nasty narrative to the kidney-stone-plagued vocals of singer Jim Rutledge as he wails his way through this corpse saga. The early 1970s was the era of the rock jam and if Bloodrock had any brains, they would've pulled a "Free Bird" and launched into an extended guitar rave-up. Instead, the song's portentous sirens, Hammond sickness (*nee-nuu nee-nuu . . .*), along with the singer's wretched scream together serve one purpose only: to creep out anybody who's listening. "DOA" isn't just depressing, it's nightmarish, and quite possibly the most evil pop single ever released.

And this, my friends, leads me to the most depressing aspect of this sick-ass tune: being forced to play it over and over again. Since "DOA" was technically Bloodrock's only "hit" single, the group found itself in a Twilight Zone nightmare as demanding audiences regularly requested to hear their charming cadaver ballad (and believe me, "DOA" is not a song you want to be saddled with under any circumstances). Bloodrock's own members, weary of waking up screaming in the middle of the night, began refusing: "We're not here to sing about death," they sniffed to audiences at their concerts. In the performance rule book written for one-hit-wonder bands, this is faux pas numero uno; it's like Chubby Checker declining to sing "The Twist" at an oldies show. Crowds walked out of Bloodrock shows en masse until, by 1974, their fans could be counted on Mickey Mouse's fingers. This, coupled with numerous personnel changes and the band's ludicrous decision to adopt a flute-driven sound à la Jethro Tull, effectively killed Bloodrock.

Still, if you ever find yourself driving through the Texas Panhandle late at night and tune into a small FM album rock station in Amarillo, then maybe, just maybe . . .

Nee-nuu nee-nuu nee-nuu nee-nuu . . .

Sylvia's Mother

Performed by Dr. Hook and the Medicine Show
Released 1972 (No. 2 in the UK, no. 5 in the US)
Words and Music by Shel Silverstein

NOWADAYS you can't turn on AM radio without hearing a right-wing radio host railing about the left-wing-dominated mainstream media. (Or is it the other way around?) But, for decades, AM was the bastion of Top 40 radio where masses of bad songs would suddenly appear in rotation and be turned into hits. Though clearly a goof, the lachrymose-sounding "Sylvia's Mother" became a worldwide smash due to constant airplay, and briefly made stars out of the silly group that performed it. Today, "Sylvia's Mother" draws bewildered reactions from listeners raised on Eminem, as if they can't believe nobody got that it was a joke when it was first released.

Long broken up and forgotten, Dr. Hook and the Medicine Show was a novelty band out of New Jersey led by the Mutt-and-Jeff pairing of Dennis Locorriere and Ray Sawyer. The band's name came from the Captain Hook–like eye patch Sawyer wore, the result of his losing an eye in a car accident. Locorriere, though, was Dr. Hook's main singer, with a gift for mimicry. Their whacky stage act led them to be partnered up with the late humorist/illustrator Shel Silverstein, known for his magazine work and children's books. Silverstein had bags of songs lying around and Dr. Hook was basically hired to perform them. Every song on the group's first four albums was written by Silverstein, including the over-the-top "Sylvia's Mother."

The Song

"Sylvia's Mother" is sung (bawled is more like it) from the perspective of a heartbroken young man who's on a payphone trying to talk to his ex-girlfriend Sylvia but, unfortunately, can't get past her mother. Everything starts off unpretentiously with an acoustic guitar, bass, and lightly brushed snare drum, though I could do without the harpsichord. "Sylvia's mother says Sylvia's busy, too busy to come to the phone," Locorriere whimpers, staring at the rotary dialer (this is 1972, remember). He learns that Sylvia's getting ready to start a new life, and she asks him to leave her alone. Suddenly, the operator cuts in and demands forty cents for the next three minutes, money he doesn't have. This sets up the song's notorious chorus where Locorriere literally has a breakdown, his voice choking up as a wave of harmony vocals surges behind him. "Please, Mrs. Avery, I just gotta talk to her," he sobs into the receiver. All he wants to do is tell her good-bye.

By now, anybody with sense enough to step around a sleeping Rottweiler would assume this whole thing is a joke. We're waiting for the punch line, the clown horn, the pie in the face . . . something. Instead, the song continues and the boy discovers that Sylvia's packing to leave town. The mother tells him that Sylvia's marrying another boy. His anxious pleadings make Sylvia's mother relent finally but she warns him to not say anything "to make her start crying and stay." Of course, that damned operator keeps cutting in demanding another forty cents. The chorus returns, "Please Mrs. Avery . . . !"

OK, everyone must've figured out this song's a joke by now. Nobody sings this overwrought without there being a huge wink and stifled laughter behind it. Unfortunately, the three-and-a-half million teenagers who bought copies of this record (seriously) were too busy blubbering to know they were being had. Locorriere goes in for the kill, having Sylvia decline to come to the phone. "She's catching the nine o'clock train," the mother tells him, before reminding her to take her umbrella. "Sylvia, it's starting to rain." Sylvia leaves and the poor guy is left with . . . Sylvia's mother. "Won't you call back again," she tells him sweetly. Then the operator, then the chorus: "Please, Mrs. Avery . . . !"

Why It's Depressing

If you can imagine this without fainting, "Sylvia's Mother" was played to death on AM radio and its worldwide success compelled the BBC to declare it the "Worst Record in the History of Pop Music" (move over "MacArthur Park"). Not surprisingly, listeners grew to despise "Sylvia's Mother," but whether or not it was a joke was another issue. The song was ambiguous enough in 1972 that even the most cynical couldn't quite figure it out; 20/20 hindsight shows that, of course, it was just a spoof of weepy teenage heartbreak songs and car crash tragedies like "Tell Laura I Love Her." But satirizing anything requires a fair amount of verisimilitude and, unfortunately, the attention to detail basically fogs the joke of "Sylvia's Mother." Locorriere really sounds shattered when he sings "Sylvia's Mother," and you can see the lonely youth clutching a receiver in a phone booth, anxiously waiting for Sylvia to talk to him. Though I was very young when I first heard it, I thought the goddamned song was serious and I've always been cynical (in my defense, I hated it because it made me feel awful the entire day). The lyrics aren't remotely funny, so the joke apparently was in the manner the group performed the song. Once people figured this out, it was too late. They spent all of 1972 getting bummed out hearing it everywhere and weren't amused to learn they were supposed to laugh.

Being their first hit single, "Sylvia's Mother" became an albatross around the collective necks of Dr. Hook and the

Medicine Show until even they hated it. They managed to score another hit with the straightforward novelty song "Cover of the Rolling Stone" but it was the band's twilight. Silverstein's songs were basically ditties and nobody would take Dr. Hook seriously. They made a brief comeback in 1976 with a bland cover of Sam Cooke's "Only Sixteen" that broke into the Top 20. The group was relegated to playing small clubs and eventually broke up in 1985.

The End

Performed by the Doors
Released 1967
Written by Jim Morrison, Robbie Krieger, Ray Manzarek,
and John Densmore

THE DOORS' place in music history lies primarily with their being the only major rock group whose lead singer was from another planet. I don't mean that in a cosmic interstellar way. I'm talking about a sci-fi B-movie with cheesy special effects, the kind of flick where you can visibly see the nylon strings on the jaw of the giant Martian robot. For years, those grainy Doors concert films featuring a skulking, entranced Jim Morrison were considered visual records of the poet/shaman in full sermon. Today, there's something creaky about them, with Morrison coming off as a hippie Godzilla tromping around like he's destroying Tokyo with the stoned audience standing in for a wide-eyed Japanese populace. But since he lucked out by dying before he could grow old and fat, Morrison's mad dog persona has grown beyond the sum of its rabid parts and bequeathed him a mythical status that supersedes who he really was: a wasted, obnoxious freak.

"The End" is the Doors' infamous magnum opus, which creeped out a new generation of listeners who heard it on the soundtrack of Francis Ford Coppola's bizarre *Apocalypse Now*. The song appears on the group's eponymous 1967 debut album, a stereo release with the instruments so separated it sounds like it was mixed according to a tidal chart ("high tide, right channel . . . low tide, left channel . . ."). More than a few pints of ink have been spilled by critics analyzing "The End," particularly the jabbering murder story that Morrison unleashes in the song's middle when he recorded it so long ago. But misty-eyed 1960s fans be damned, I'm calling this droning one-chord hypno-fest for what it is: a druggy epic horror.

The Song

The best way to examine "The End" is via step-by-step instructions on reproducing it the way the Doors did inside the Whiskey A Go-Go forty years ago. All you need is a D-minor chord and a lead singer who's loaded up on LSD. Guitarists, tune your low sixth string down a full step (E to D) and fret a first position D minor chord, the same one R.E.M. used to build their career with. Play around with it, but don't forget to add the C# on the second string for that raga-tinged harmonic minor sound. You've now written 98 percent of this song.

Since this is your music, you the guitarist must include some lyrics. You have some verses you wrote about the end of a relationship: "This is the end, beautiful friend, the end. This is the end, my only friend, the end . . ." This is the extent of the lyrics you wrote. Give them to your lead singer. Keep in mind you just met him six months earlier and haven't decided whether he's a genius or an ax murderer.

"It's called 'The End,'" you tell him, handing him a lyric sheet.

"Who let all these bats in here?" he mumbles, waving his hand above his head.

You, the drummer, and the egghead keyboardist who brought this maniac into the group will start playing around with the D-minor chord. The result should be an eerie droning vamp, music you'd listen to while changing religions.

Next, book yourself at the Whiskey A Go-Go on LA's fabulous Sunset Strip. It's a go-go club; it must be because it has the word Go-Go on the marquee. Go onstage with your one-chord song and begin playing it. Silently hope what's-his-face has some more lyrics. "C'mon, you're the big poet," you think. "This is the end," he sings in a Summer of Love croon, while gazing off with the same dazed expression a spaniel has after licking its balls. Suddenly, he'll respond to some subconscious cue, mournfully wailing about "what will be, so limitless and free . . ." References to "stranger's hands" and "a desperate land" spew forth. "Wow," you'll think, "that's pretty deep. I don't know what it means but, hey, we worked in two more chords." As the crowd watches your singer chew on the linoleum, you'll feel inspired. Explore all the dark crevices of your D-minor chord (note: There are about four, six if you take enough drugs). Learn to love D minor; it's the only chord you'll be playing for the next three hours.

Your ersatz Hindu music should grow and expand until it sounds like Boddisattva and Vishnu starting a war over curry. Have your singer climb further up the free-association ladder until he's up where geese fly. "All the children are insaaannne," he moans, grabbing the microphone in a chicken-strangling grip. The crowd will look at him the way people do when they see a UFO. "The blue bus is calling us . . ." Feel relieved that this is still the 1960s.

Now a moment happens that nobody anticipated, including you. Your singer will go into a trance and begin babbling: "The killer awoke before dawn. He put his shoes on . . ." "OK, what the hell is this?" you'll think, taking two steps back. The crowd will take two steps back. Cops patrolling the Strip will change lanes. Your singer tells a rambling story about a killer walking around his house visiting his sister's room, then his brother's to do God knows what before loudly bellowing, "then he WALKED on down the hall!!" By now, the crowd should be crawling under the tables to take cover.

Your singer will be building to the climax of his tale, where the killer enters his parents' bedroom. He'll shriek an expletive at the top of his lungs, which implies having carnal relations with mom. Watch the blood drain out of the club manager's face. Watch the crowd do a mass duck-and-cover. Watch your singer turn into a gecko. Panicking, you bash away hard on your D-minor chord until your guitar feeds back. "Kill . . . Kill . . . Kill . . . Kill . . ." your singer chants. After you hit a crescendo normally reserved for cannon barrages, bring the music back down to its pianissimo level. Repeat the opening verses about how this is the end. Trust me, the audience will believe it. The song should end quietly while your singer swigs from a pint of rubbing alcohol. Have the club's manager storm up and tell you that you're fired. Three months later, become rock 'n' roll stars.

Why It's Depressing

Listening to "The End" is like staring at a whale-sized Rorschach ink blot: People may have different reactions about what it means, but they'll all agree there's an awful lot of black space. It's one of those songs that always sounds longer than it actually is. Perhaps that's the intent since drug trips are perpetual experiences that don't punch a time clock. It wasn't unusual for bands of the Doors' era to pick a single chord and go wandering around the cosmos, but "The End" dollops on so much dark imagery that even your CD player gets winded playing it. One of Jim Morrison's biggest talents was his innate ability to make everything he coughed up extemporaneously seem profound. Yes, he had "a way with words," as the saying goes, but when it came to linking thoughts together, Morrison's attention span went elsewhere. Trends in modern art help excuse most of the Lizard King's lapses, using buzzwords like "imagist" and "non-linear" to rationalize the ramblings of an otherwise intelligent guy who spent the last the seven years of his life whacked out of his mind. It doesn't help that Coppola used "The End" to bookend *Apocalypse Now*. Does anybody really want their song associated with napalm and a tubby Marlon Brando? Though

"The End" had nothing to do with Vietnam, the song is strongly associated with the most depressing war film ever made, as well as bad acid trips, matricide, desolated landscapes, and one-chord songs that last an eternity. For those who've never heard it, you should listen to "The End" once. It won't kill you but you may not be able to resist the urge to scream for somebody to change chords, fer chrissakes. Have fun.

I Had No Idea That Song Was So Morbid

Alone Again (Naturally)

Written and performed by Gilbert O'Sullivan
Released 1972 (No. 3 in the UK, no. 1 in the US)

"HEY, Paul McCartney has a new song out," radio listeners remarked when a bouncy piano-driven single entitled "Alone Again (Naturally)" first hit the airwaves in 1972. This misconception was quickly cleared up when, twenty-five seconds into it, the singer announced that he was going to throw himself off a tower. "Wait a minute," people said, "that's not Paul McCartney. Who is this guy and why's he ruining my day?"

The guy was Gilbert O'Sullivan, a diminutive Irish singer-songwriter who inexplicably hit number one in the United States with "Alone Again (Naturally)," a musically ebullient yet fatalistic song about a depressed man who's been jilted on his wedding day. It's the only composition not written by Paul McCartney that still sounds like he wrote it, then chucked it aside, muttering, "What the bejeezus was I thinking?" O'Sullivan had recorded unsuccessfully for a few years until he was taken under the wing of music manager and record label owner Gordon Mills, the man who oversaw the careers of Tom Jones and Englebert Humperdinck; he later sued Mills to get out of a draconian record contract and was awarded back royalties and the rights to all his master recordings. The success of "Alone Again (Naturally)," along with the fact that he was a pianist, made many people at the time consider O'Sullivan a serious rival to another new pop sensation: Elton John. This comparison proved to be specious because:

(a) Gilbert O'Sullivan never repeated the success of this song.

(b) the public still hasn't forgiven him for this song.

The Song

I've always been intrigued by songs with downer lyrics, upbeat music, and no explanation for this incongruity. On first listen, "Alone Again (Naturally)" sounds catchy enough and you're quite certain you're hearing a song about a guy having some "alone time" with his best girl. But no, this guy really is alone. As the piano pumps along in its faux–Leon Russell manner, O'Sullivan sings a first-person account of a guy who's standing at the altar wearing an ill-fitting rented tux and realizing his bride-to-be isn't showing up anytime soon. The guests are clucking their tongues, saying "My God, that's tough, she stood him up." Not feeling too keen at the moment, the groom declares he's going to throw himself off the nearest tower if only to show everyone what it feels like "when you're shattered." The fact that everyone's already barreled out of the church like Posh Spice fleeing the paparazzi creates a sticky problem, like the tree-falling-in-the-woods question: If a man openly threatens suicide and there's no one around to hear it, is he really serious?

In the case of this guy, probably not. He's merely a self-pitying type who sounds like a Michelin going flat every time he sighs. He goes into a funk for an entire week if his latte doesn't have enough foam. We know he's "alone again, naturally," because he's used to it. Why else would he keep repeating it throughout the song? The adverb "naturally" speaks volumes. He claims he was looking forward to his impending nuptials but then "reality came around" and "cut me into little pieces." Now he's cursing God for deserting him in his hour of need. The piano merrily plunks away. The world is filled with more broken hearts than could ever be mended, he intones while staring at the empty pews, "What do we do? What do we do?" This should be where the tune ends but, like many a depressing songwriter, O'Sullivan cannot resist driving an extra nail into our skulls.

It is now years later and the jilted groom is telling us about the death of his parents. "Why in heaven's name are you talking about that?" you want to scream. It's probably because that's who he was living with when they kicked. First Dad passes on, leaving Mom and her feckless son behind. Then she passes, leaving her son behind. God is such a bastard. "Alone again," he declares, "naturally."

Why It's Depressing

Everybody can identify with feeling beaten down by a failed relationship, and getting left at the altar is certainly humiliating. The problem with "Alone Again (Naturally)" is the song's protagonist. Most of us have met guys like him. You can find them in bookstores at 11 P.M. on a Friday flipping through Nietzsche anthologies. They think the movie *Trainspotting* is too upbeat. They think Nine Inch Nails is too upbeat. They do office temp work while penning unreadable screenplays in their spare time, which are 40 percent dream sequences. The man is an exhausting schlemiel who went through his entire adolescence with a "Kick me" sign taped to his back. Now grown, his sullen, mumbling personality has been mistaken for being "deep and introspective" by a wide-eyed girl who met him in a coffee shop while he was hunched over his latest script thinking, "How would a dwarf say this?" Within a month, they get engaged.

By the time the big day arrives, though, the bride realizes she's about to marry an erratically employed drip whose biggest accomplishment is being able to quote the first four lines of T. S. Eliot's "The Wasteland" from memory. "I'm outta here," she says, leaving him "standing in the lurch at a church," which, truth be told, is subconsciously what he hoped would happen because it helps confirm his misanthropic see-I-told-you-so view of the world. This is who the song is about and, as much as you want to sympathize, guys like him suck all the energy out of a limbo party.

Artificial Flowers

Performed by Bobby Darin
Released 1960 (No. 20 in the US)
Written by Jerry Bock and Sheldon Harnick

THROUGHOUT pop music's shaggy dog history, performers who scored a hit record often tried to sustain their success by releasing follow-up singles in the approximate style of their predecessors (i.e., they sound the same). It well served groups like the Beach Boys early in their career until Brian Wilson went batty and started dumping sand in his living room. But sometimes adhering to a musical paradigm leads to bizarre results, never more so than with Bobby Darin's 1960 recording of "Artificial Flowers," an up-tempo swinger about an impoverished orphan girl who freezes to death in a squalid flat.

"Artificial Flowers" has a very odd story behind it, if only because it makes no sense. Apparently, the song is meant to be a joke. Or not. See, nobody knows for sure because irony was not a popular concept in 1960 and songs about children dying of exposure typically aren't very funny. The Broadway songwriting team of Jerry Bock and Sheldon Harnick (*Fiddler on the Roof*) included "Artificial Flowers" in their musical *Tenderloin*, set in New York City's seamy Tenderloin district during the 1890s. In the first act, a cynical reporter who covers the Tenderloin as part of his beat regales a crusading minister about the hardships of the area. He sings an intentionally melodramatic ballad about a poor orphan who eked out a meager living making artificial flowers for society ladies. She ends up dying with her scissors frozen in her tiny hands. Ha ha, chuckle chuckle. Unfortunately, audiences didn't laugh so the pit band gradually sped up the tempo, thinking this would make the song funny, though the cast wasn't even sure if it was supposed to be funny. Audiences still didn't laugh. With more people leaning to the "not funny" side, the explanation for "Artificial Flowers" was that it was an imitation of Victorian-era sob songs. When nobody bought that explanation, it was said to be a parody of them. Now, forty-five years later, "Artificial Flowers" can be summed up this way: It may or may not be a funny song (that was never funny to begin with) that parodies a long-forgotten song style while paying tribute to it at the same time. (Incidentally, *Tenderloin* had a very short run on Broadway.)

Meanwhile, Bobby Darin was looking to record another song in the vein of his swinging previous hits "Beyond The Sea" and "Mack the Knife." That in itself wasn't a bad idea because if Bobby Darin was going to copy himself, it might as well be those tunes; reworking "Splish Splash" would be grounds for an indictment. What makes his version of "Artificial Flowers" so depressingly nutso is that Darin somehow bought the whole this-song-is-just-a-joke ruse and recorded it in full up-tempo finger-snapping glory.

The Song

"Artificial Flowers" begins in Darin's I'm-not-a-rocker-anymore style with an ensemble of big band musicians laying down a swingin' beat while chirping flutes undercoat everything in a layer of Vegas schmaltz. The music is so sanguine and lounge-heavy, you can practically smell the Smirnoff and you're waiting for Bobby to launch into the further adventures of Mack the Knife. Instead, we learn about poor little Ann (or Annie, as she is alternately called), a sweet nine-year-old girl whose parents went to their "final reward," leaving her behind to fend for herself. Darin never explains how Annie's mom and dad met their demise, but given the inauspicious events that follow, let's just say they were eaten by a giant squid.

From here on, the whole scenario becomes very Dickensian, with Ann serving as the neglected street orphan whose only talent is an uncanny ability to make artificial flowers "for ladies of fashion to wear." But they're not just some rote-assembled floral knock-offs; these artificial flowers, as stated in the chorus, are "fashioned from Annie's despair." The girl is quite meticulous in her handiwork, spending long hours alone in her drafty, unheated room using paper, wire, and melted wax to create veritable bouquets of tulips and mums. Naturally, Ann earns only a few measly pennies from her arduous work, peddling her papier mâché creations on the cold streets to heartless society crones on their way to one of Mrs. Astor's society balls. As most nine-year-olds go into cardiac arrest if they have to make their beds, Li'l Annie's wretched dedication to her craft means she's either a victim of child slave labor or the world's youngest obsessive-compulsive.

Any hope for salvation is for naught. As Darin croons away in his suave neo-hip manner, we learn that snow is drifting, nay, piling, into poor Annie's frigid flat as she toils away ceaselessly making more flowers. The orphan girl slowly expires from hypothermia, her "baby little fingers" losing all sense of feeling. The next morning, Annie is found frozen to death still clutching her scissors, her body covered in ice among the half-finished flowers that were "watered from all her young tears."

Darin attempts to rescue us from the horror of Annie's popsicle send-off by contemplating the possibility that she's now up in heaven frolicking in sprawling gardens while adorned in a garland of genuine flowers, not those cursed artificial ones, though after a life that sucked as much as hers she'd probably prefer a footman who resembles Brad Pitt. The song heads into a patented showroom finale, with the horns braying and the rhythm section pushing the tempo. "Throw away those arti-fi-cial flowers," Bobby wails, "those dumb dumb flow-ers . . . fashioned from Annie's des-paaaiiiiiir!" The best part of this faux-Sinatra death jazz song is right after the band blasts its final augmented ninth chord, when Darin ad libs: "Give her the real thing." It's too hep for words.

Why It's Depressing

By all accounts, Bobby Darin was a smart, ambitious man, so it's difficult to explain away "Artificial Flowers." Either he was totally fooled or simply sang off the wrong cue sheet because there ain't no way the lyrics go with the music. The Grateful Dead's Bob Weir has performed "Artificial Flowers" with his side group Ratdog on occasion, singing it in the poignant way it was originally written (when it was supposed to be funny). Darin's version sounds like he's the butt of the world's biggest musical joke. You have lyrics about a street urchin straight out of a Theodore Dreiser novel put to music that's so hipster-cool, it makes Nelson Riddle sound like Bauhaus. At best, the two should neutralize each other, like acid and alkali, but instead they serve the Greater Evil by working together to disarm listeners before bludgeoning them into a coma. Listening to "Artificial Flowers" is not unlike lunching outside a Tuscan villa with Hannibal Lecter: Everything is so pleasant and halcyon that you're unaware the smiling man seated across from you is two seconds away from tearing out your spleen.

I'm letting Bobby Darin off the hook with this bewildering song, though. Unlike today, where singers need a week's notice before they'll clear their throat, songs were banged out pretty quickly in Darin's time, often several per day. His biographers have explained away "Artificial Flowers" by saying Darin always knew the song was a joke, if indeed it was meant to be a joke. Which it may have been. Or not. My theory is that he just wasn't paying attention. Finding himself late for dinner with Sandra Dee and one song short, he absently grabbed the next tune off the pile, ordered the orchestra to "swing it hard, fellas," and launched into "alone in the world was poor little Ann . . ."

It was only three days later that he looked up from his linguini and clams and went, "Wait a minute . . ."

Indiana Wants Me

Written and performed by R. Dean Taylor
Released 1971 (No. 2 in the UK, no. 5 in the US)

"INDIANA WANTS me," R. Dean Taylor mournfully sang in 1971, "Lord, I can't go back there . . ." He may as well go back because every other state in the Union will likely throw him out knowing he brought this dreadful tune along with him. A depressing fugitive-on-the-run tale, "Indiana Wants Me" briefly topped the American charts before dropping off, apparently taking R. Dean Taylor's career along with it.

To my ears, this otherwise dreary record is remarkable for one single aspect: R. Dean Taylor sounds so much like Simon and Garfunkel on "Mrs. Robinson," it's amazing he never got sued.

Taylor was a white Canadian who worked as a songwriter for Berry Gordy's Motown label before launching a singing career (he penned, among other things, the notorious "Love Child" for the Supremes). After scoring a minor hit in England with the song "Gotta See Jane," Taylor released "Indiana Wants Me" to an American record-buying public hungry for songs with revolutionary themes and they snapped it up under the erroneous impression it was something anthemic, another "American Pie" or "What's Goin' On." What they got instead was a song about a recalcitrant prick who goes on the run after killing a guy who insulted his wife.

The Song

"Indiana Wants Me" begins its fugitive narrative in the clumsiest way possible: police sirens. This is not good. This is bad, very bad. *Pet Sounds* and *Sgt. Pepper* aside, sound effects on records are the jurisdiction of Spike Jonze and his novelty ilk. You cannot possibly take anything seriously that follows, starting with the song's marriage of Paul and Art harmonies with the road movie vibe of "Me and Bobby McGee." It hooks us in with its hokey (though undeniably catchy) chorus, with which Taylor beats the listener over the head throughout the song. Since Indiana was after him, many Vietnam-era listeners assumed it was for something political like staging a sit-in outside the entrance to an ROTC recruiting office in Muncie. But, no, he's just a guy who bolts after murdering a man who supposedly spoke ill of his better half. As is common in depressing songs, we never learn the specifics of what the slander was; maybe he said her shoes didn't match her belt. The only thing we know is that if anyone deserved to die, "he did."

Taylor's fugitive is clearly a hair-trigger type, one of those white-trash denizens who gets busted every week on *COPS* for having a meth lab inside his mobile home. Now he's on the run, hiding in haystacks and filching rides from truckers hauling down the I-30. From here on, our wanted man is filled with regrets, having quickly learned that the fugitive life sucks rocks. Cold and lonely, he endures a panicked existence while everyone is out hunting for him. "It hurts to see the man that I've become," he laments, scribbling his ramblings in a message to his wife. "I'll never see your smiling face or touch your hand." The errant bad boy seeks redemption by asking her to forgive him for *ruining her life* (italics mine) and urges her to hold on to memories of their "happy years" together (and those were . . . ?). The wife, at home with their colicky baby and a tapped phone, reads through the letter while finally understanding why her parents disowned her after she married this misfit.

Like all tragedies, there is no happy ending to Taylor's saga as the law finally catches up with the wanted man while he's dashing off his latest missive. A wall of wailing sirens right out of a 1930s gangster movie comes pouring in along with the bull-horned voice of an audio engineer, er, cop, telling him he's surrounded. By now you're praying the guy pulls a Butch and Sundance and charges out with guns ablazin' just so the police will have an excuse to drill him. They evidently do, judging by the hilarious ricocheting gunshots that erupt during the song's fade, sounding like Deputy Dawg and Quick Draw McGraw restaging the climax to *High Noon*.

Why It's Depressing

Songs about criminals and bad men are problematic. They require the anti-hero personas of a John Wesley Harding or Stagger Lee, mythical outlaws who can be folded into any storyline since their biographies are too arcane and sepia-toned to contradict anything (Stagger Lee shot Billy Lyons for [insert reason here]). Otherwise, you end up flailing at the bottom of the desperado ballad pit alongside the loser of "Indiana Wants Me." The ordeal of this nut job does not warrant a Tom Dooley–like request for redemption since he's clearly the type who smacks his missus around, gets fired from every job, and skips out on bar tabs. His howling regret over a misspent life sounds like so much empty whining and, if given another chance, he'd be on the run again, this time for knifing the referee at the local cockfights after he ruled against his favorite rooster.

I'm convinced that listeners at the time were entranced by the song's catchy chorus, which probably had a cool anti-establishment ring to their naïve ears. It was only after repeatedly listening to the song that its full narrative became apparent: Guy kills other guy, guy flees, guy dies. By that time, they'd already bought the single and realized they'd been screwed.

I Mope,

therefore

I Am

Prayers for Rain

Performed by the Cure
Released 1989
Written by Robert Smith, Simon Gallop, Roger O'Donnell,
Porl Thompson, Lol Tolhurst, and Boris Williams

WHEN FRIENDS of mine found out I was writing a book on depressing music, they inevitably said, "Oh, you mean like the Cure?" It seems more than a little obvious to include a Cure tune in a book devoted to spirit-crushing songs, but that presents a serious challenge. Selecting the most depressing Cure song is like choosing your favorite locust in a locust swarm: You pretty much have your pick, but does it really make any difference?

Having never really gotten into the Cure but being acutely aware of their glum-meister reputation, I set out to explore the group's onyx-hued world by listening to every one of their albums, beginning with 1980's *Seventeen Seconds*. By the time I got through 1989's *Disintegration*, I was dressing like Nosferatu and sneaking into farms to suck the blood out of cattle. I'd never heard more nightmarishly fucked-up music in my life and came away convinced that frontman Robert Smith sleeps in a coffin surrounded by empty absinthe bottles and the drained corpses of young virgins. Along the way, I noticed that one particular Cure song had latched on to me like leprosy. It was "Prayers for Rain" from the aforementioned *Disintegration*, easily one of the most depressing albums ever released. Others may disagree ("All Cats Are Gray" and "The Drowning Man" came highly recommended), but I'm confident that "Prayers for Rain" is the bleakest of Robert Smith's oeuvre, which readily makes it one of the world's bleakest.

The Song

"Prayers for Rain" begins like practically every Cure song, with an introduction that's longer than most Bo Diddley singles. Never mind the omnipresent chill, why does Robert Smith write such interminable intros? I can put on "Prayers for Rain," then cook an omelette in the time it takes him to start singing. He seems to have a rule that the creepier the song, the longer the wait before it actually starts. I'm not sure if Smith spends the intro time applying eye-liner or manually reducing his serotonin level, but one must endure a lot of doom-filled guitar patterns, cathedral-reverb drums, and modal string synth wanderings during the opening of "Prayers for Rain." Musically, it's classic Cure, all portentous and fundamental. Smith loves minor keys the way Samuel Beckett loved futility, and the band lumbers back and forth between two menacing chords like Frankenstein deciding which villager to pummel. The entire song, all six minutes and eight seconds of it, never leaves its murky roost, which gives Smith a rote harmonic base on which he can go catatonic.

As far as the lyrics go, the following list contains most of the words in "Prayers for Rain":

> shatter
> dull
> kill
> stifle
> infectious
> hopelessness
> rain
> suffocate
> dirt
> nowhere

desolate
drab
killing
fracture
stale
strangle
entangle
deteriorate
drearily
tired

Now just drop in the pronouns "I" and "You," plus a few prepositions and conjunctions, and you have "Prayers for Rain" in its entirety. There's no story or narrative, just a lot of pewter-gray imagery and toxic metaphors. Like Billy Joel in his ponderous "Captain Jack," Smith sings "Prayers for Rain" entirely in the second person, where "you" the listener are the one behind all the shattering, stifling, suffocating, and killing being inflicted upon him. (It's apparent that he's addressing some boon companion of his who happens to be a raving psychotic.) "You shatter me . . . you strangle me . . . you fracture me . . ." are among the litany of accustions Smith harps on in the song, the results being "I suffocate, I breathe in dirt." As is the norm, Smith sings in that neurotic bleating voice of his that always sounds like he just got punched in the stomach after eating a three-course meal. "Desolate and drab, the hours all spent . . ." is how he describes his life, one that is barely made more tolerable with "prayers for rain." The merriness and warmth never end.

Little nuggets of interest appear, however. There is actually a bridge of sorts, where the group ingeniously adds yet another Black Death chord to their riffing while repeating the second set of verses. I personally like the demented analog synthesizer line that creeps around the song like a violin ensemble staffed with roaches. Love the backward piano loops, too (nightingales flying into a brick wall). The song ends with a flurry of reverse piano figures whipping around, as if the entire bird flock just soared into the Transamerica building.

Why It's Depressing

While gritting my teeth through "Prayers for Rain," I was struck by how long it is. Many Cure songs, in fact, are seven minutes or more in length while not featuring any musical arcs. Harmonically, "Prayers for Rain" has all the hills and valleys of the Bonneville Salt Flats while possessing the dynamics of a golem's eulogy. Even for a Cure tune, the song is so oppressive, it borders on manic. It never moves beyond "you [bad verb] me" and therefore "I [worse verb]" which leads to "I breathe/eat dirt." "Prayers for Rain" sounds more like the rant of someone in a twelve-step program having a "breakthrough" (or a breakdown) than a song. Yes, the engineering is ace and the playing expert but, God, enough already. Seriously, Robert, we get it, OK?

I know I'm offending goths everywhere who would prefer I took my Stevie Ray Vaughan albums and shoved them but, seriously, how do you deal with a group whose leader looks like Edward Scissorhands? I think the best way to describe "Prayers for Rain" (besides AUUUUUGGGGGGGGGHHH!!!) is that it's a musical palindrome. If Smith sang this song backward, it would sound the same and you'd still feel compelled to throw yourself into a nest of adders.

Sister Morphine

Originally performed by Marianne Faithfull
Released 1969 (remade in 1979)
Also performed by the Rolling Stones
Released 1971
Words and music by Marianne Faithfull, Mick Jagger,
and Keith Richards

A SONG with a title like "Sister Morphine" would normally be consigned to another category in this book, but when the songwriter's an actual junkie, the bar is, unfortunately, raised. Genuine addicts are held in high regard in the music industry and the more confessional the better. "Sister Morphine" was made famous by the Rolling Stones when it appeared on their superlative 1971 album *Sticky Fingers*, but what many don't know is that the song's lyrics were cowritten by Marianne Faithfull, the 1960s icon cum Stones girlfriend cum heroin addict who happens to possess the most depressing female singing voice this side of Nico.

The turbulent life of Marianne Faithfull is well documented. Discovered at eighteen by Rolling Stones manager Andrew Loog Oldham, she scored a Top 10 hit in England in 1964 with her eerie cover of "As Tears Go By," which Mick Jagger and Keith Richards wrote for her. (To this day, it's still a disturbing record to hear.) Beautiful and fragile, Faithfull became Jagger's paramour and the two were the royal couple of London's swinging 1960s scene. A notorious drug bust in 1967 at Keith Richards's house scotched her singing career, but two years later she released a single called "Something Better" whose B-side contained her original version of "Sister Morphine," cowritten with Jagger and Richards. Within days, it was yanked from record store shelves all across England. By the end of the decade, she was a full-time needle fiend with a serious heroin problem. After attempting suicide, she broke up with Jagger and ended up homeless on the streets of London, completely strung out. In short, Faithfull suffered most of the pitfalls that her "Sister Morphine" lyrics warn against and, while her versions aren't as good as the Rolling Stones', they're far more debilitating.

The Song

"Sister Morphine" is usually labeled an anti-drug song (a "stark" one, of course) and deciding which version was more depressing was tricky for me. I had to take into account who's a bigger mess: Marianne Faithfull or Keith Richards. In the end, she "won," if only because Richards still plays guitar as well as he ever did while Faithfull's voice is basically shot. By the time she rerecorded "Sister Morphine" in 1979 (a far more polished version than the rough-hewn original), her trademark wounded soprano had long turned into a guttural alto growl from years of hard living. Naturally, critics prefer her damaged voice, which just emphasizes the bad voice = serious artist equation.

"Here I lie," she moans, after an ominous crashing of cymbals and minor-chorded Fender guitar gets us into the clinic with her. The song takes place entirely in a hospital bed (shades of Metallica's "One") with the patient, in this case Ms. Faithfull, inquiring when "Sister Morphine" is coming around to see her again. We don't know why she's in the hospital but I'm guessing Sister Morphine has something to do with it. She's obviously in great pain as she insists "I don't think I can wait," because her strength is failing. The band kicks in, settling into an uneasy yet funky groove that sounds oddly seductive, while Faithfull has the usual addict flashbacks. She recalls a ride in an ambulance, the "scream" of a siren, and a doctor who has "no face." At the end of the second stanza, she desperately wants to score.

It's important to remember that Marianne Faithfull did not rely on her own personal experiences when she cowrote "Sister Morphine" because most of them hadn't happened yet. (Supposedly, Faithfull only used heroin once before writing the lyrics.) This isn't wise because if you're going to write a confessional song about, say, cutting your hand off with an ax, make sure you write it after you do the severing. In Faithfull's case, she got the creative process back-to-front. The addiction, overdoses, suicide attempts, withdrawals, hospital stays, and faceless doctors portrayed in "Sister Morphine" afflicted her in the years following the song's release.

The second half of the song is very much like the first (OK, it's exactly like the first) as Faithfull repeats her pathetic cries for "Sister Morphine" to turn her "nightmares into dreams" while claiming once again that she's dying. One more shot will be her "last." It sounds very convincing but she starts sounding a tad greedy when she asks "Sweet Cousin Cocaine" to help cool off her head. (The familial references to hard drugs are a little much, don'tcha think?) None of this matters because Faithfull has given up on living and only asks that Sister Morphine make her bed after she's gone. "You can sit around," she rasps, inviting everyone to watch as all her "clean white sheets turn red."

The track slowly fades out, the band too numb to go any further.

Why It's Depressing

People suffering from drug withdrawal make for dreary subject matter and I've yet to find any song that surpasses "Sister Morphine" for sheer self-pity; all she wants to do is get a fix, then die. That alone will tempt you to drop a safe on your head, but the most depressing aspect of "Sister

Morphine" is Faithfull's broken voice. Never a great singer, her craggy vocal work on all her albums since the 1970s is an acquired taste, and the trashed quality of her vocal on "Sister Morphine" is quite pitiful. Yes, she sounds like a junkie but, by that token, she sounds like a junkie on every song she sings. Grim as it may be, the Rolling Stones' version of "Sister Morphine" redeems itself with sublime dynamics, a bluesy romp and stunning slide guitar work from guest Ry Cooder. Faithfull's version is more straightforward yet curiously gloomier. Her band, though excellent players, handicap themselves by employing a vamping accompaniment that can only be described as the saddest groove ever played.

Marianne Faithfull is a survivor, no question about it, and I don't deny her place in the annals of Stonesology but her story is more about lost opportunities and vanished youth. That she helped write "Sister Morphine" before experiencing all the dire consequences addressed in the song is telling. Why couldn't she have taken her own advice and laid off the spike? Did she want to sing like Nico that badly?

Hurt

Performed by Nine Inch Nails
Released 1995 (No. 8 in the US)
Performed by Johnny Cash
Released 2003 (No. 39 in the UK, no. 33 in the US)
Words and Music by Trent Reznor

THOUGH I pillory several big-name artists for their insufferable remakes of other people's songs, sometimes the concept gets reversed where the remake is better than the original. Everyone knows that Jimi Hendrix's version of Bob Dylan's "All Along the Watchtower" blows the original out of the water, while Nirvana bested David Bowie with their unplugged rendition of his "The Man Who Sold the World." And let's not forget Hilary and Haley Duff's cover of the Go-Gos' "Our Lips Are Sealed" which . . . never mind, scratch that.

It's important to note that Dylan's and Bowie's originals weren't bad at all—both had their eccentric charm—but it is rare when someone makes a memorable remake of a song by an artist whose original version chomps the rusty bar. I'm referring to Johnny Cash's outstanding cover of the painful Nine Inch Nails song "Hurt." While I acknowledge NIN's Trent Reznor his musical talent and production savvy, the guy wouldn't know fun if it knocked on his door dressed up as a goth chick. The man has made a career entertaining serial killers in training with his barren screamings and, if I wanted to be lazy, I would've devoted this entire book to Reznor's songs because, let's face it, they're all depressing. He is the lord of despair, the guru of doom, the avatar of alienation, yay for him. The guy really needs to lighten the hell up.

The late, great Johnny Cash, on the other hand, was an American treasure and a lover of stories. A whole new generation of music fans rediscovered the Man in Black via his work with producer Rick Rubin and the marvelous American Recordings series, featuring Cash doing solo acoustic performances of traditional ballads along with contemporary songs by Soundgarden, Depeche Mode, and U2. In 2002, he released one of his last albums, *The Man Comes Around*, which features his haunting version of "Hurt."

The Song

For anyone wishing to understand the difference between a depressing song and a sad song, there's no better example than "Hurt." Reznor's version is depressing; Cash's remake is sad. The original appeared on NIN's dispiriting 1994 album *The Downward Spiral*, the perfect CD to crank up while you're throwing live hamsters into a blender. The song clocks in at over six minutes with a strident, windy hiss running through the entire track. (Reznor has a weakness for howling, screeching, ambient noises on much of his work, as if to emphasize his industrial rock rep, lest anyone forget.)

The lyrics, admittedly effective, are sung from the point of view of a heroin addict taking stock of his miserable life. "I hurt myself today," Reznor says in a tortured whisper over an oddly chorded guitar (B minor with an augmented eleventh, if anyone cares). The addict is so numb that he inflicts pain on himself just to feel anything at all. He tries to block out the tortured feeling but cannot: "I remember everything."

As the music switches to an intense pulse, Reznor contemplates what he's become, noticing how everyone around him "goes away in the end." He then launches into an anguished cry, saying how he's willing to give up everything, "my empire of dirt," then adds how no one should ever count on him for anything. He promises to always let us down.

So far, so horrid. We are in the midst of the most self-loathing drug addiction song since the Velvet Underground's "Heroin" minus Lou Reed's deadpan delivery. We're shown just how rotten everything is because he can't repair all the broken thoughts in his head, and his feelings have vanished over time. Reznor repeats the chorus while trying to keep his appendix from rupturing, all the while relishing the line "my empire of dir-rt!"

When he wishes he could start all over again somewhere else, the vocals are literally buried in an avalanche of guitar feedback and more industrial howls. The wave of sustained grinding lasts for more than a minute (which is a long time) until it abruptly cuts off, leaving us with the hissing static that opened the song. After hearing it, you need a penicillin shot.

Why It's Depressing

Reznor commits the error made by so many thrash/industrial/hardcore/death metal/whatever outfits where they feel they must hang shrunken-head necklaces around the necks of their flesh-eating zombies. Such excessive attention to redundant details threatens to turn the overall picture into parody. I'm sure there's a no-holds-barred rationale for this, but the truth is it's aggravating. Fans of NIN have never been bothered by Reznor's tortured performances but, then again, does anything bother them? The whole concept of nuance is as foreign to them as stage-diving is to Jessica Simpson.

The reason I'm being so harsh is that underneath all the groaning compressor noises and whispered angst of NIN's "Hurt" is a powerful and melodic song. This is what Johnny Cash understood, and his stripped-down version featuring two acoustic guitars, one piano, and zero diesel engines goes directly to the broken soul of "Hurt." He delivers a devastatingly moving performance that quite frankly eclipses the original. You cannot listen to it without your heart coming out of your mouth, and it's proof how sometimes it takes an interpreter to articulate the message.

For a truly cathartic reaction, watch the music video of "Hurt." A weary, elderly Johnny Cash sits surrounded by mementoes of his long career as he sings the song, while film clips of himself as a young, lean outlaw flash by. The drug theme is transformed into a nostalgic reflection of a life that touched so many others yet leaves the man himself questioning whether he meant anything at all.

He did.

Women's Prison

Performed by Loretta Lynn
Released 2004
Words and Music by Loretta Lynn

THE PAUCITY of country titles in this book might seem odd when you consider Nashville's legacy of putting out music that makes you want to arrange your own funeral. The legendary Loretta Lynn alone has recorded dozens of memorably depressing songs and, as with the Cure, this makes choosing her most spirit-breaking one a challenge of Sisyphus-like proportions. I listened to her classic hits like "The Darkest Day," "God Gave Me a Heart to Forgive," and, of course, "The Pill" (which isn't really depressing but is a riot) and found a wealth of quality misery-laden songs. But I wanted to rise to the challenge, so I set out to find something even better. I started at the beginning of her career and worked forward, but as it turned out I should've done the reverse and gone backward. It would've saved a lot of time because I discovered Loretta Lynn recorded one of country music's all-time most depressing songs in 2004: "Women's Prison."

The song is off her album *Van Lear Rose*, which received a fair amount of ink because of her collaboration with type-A guitarist and White Stripes leader Jack White, who produced it. His guttural hollow-body electric guitar drives every track on the album, all of them written by Loretta. *Van Lear Rose* received bushels of critical raves, though after listening to it, it's clear that when it comes to country music, Jack White doesn't know jack. Much of the album sounds like Loretta is singing on a White Stripes album, albeit one with better drumming. Still, working with someone so edgy undoubtedly had an effect on her, inspiring her to pen the fatalistic "Women's Prison," a song that sets her smack in the middle of Death Row on the very day she's to face Old Sparky.

The Song

One of the charms of country music is how unapologetic the songs are. They freely use the same themes and stock characters over and over again, the very ones that are used to lampoon the music. With "Women's Prison" we have all the standard country-song archetypes, including a honky tonk, a darlin' who's cheatin', gunplay, mama, and, of course, prison. No guy in a country song ever gets caught by his wife at the office bending his secretary over the Xerox machine. Couples never go to therapy or enroll in twelve-step programs. Somewhere out there, there's a speakeasy that is the site of the 5,000 murders committed in country songs so far.

Over White's doomed booming guitar, Loretta sings, "I'm in a women's prison with bars all around . . ." It seems she caught her "darlin' cheatin" with her best friend in a honky tonk and took it upon herself to shoot him. There's no dreary exposition, no recollection of happier times, no how-could-you hand wringing, just *BAM*! One more cowboy lying sprawled on the pool table.

"The judge says I'm guilty, my sentence is to die," she continues. (This judgment is so quick and harsh I'm guessing she shot her darlin' in Texas.) The music cranks along with subdued rim shots and an organ filling in the spaces while a steel guitarist feebly tries to make a country song out of the proceedings. When the drums kick in during the chorus, you know he's failed. Loretta sings about the screaming crowd, letting us know her darlin' had a large extended family that wants revenge for shooting their only kinfolk who was actually employed. But over all the noise she adds, "I can hear my mama cry." If you listen to enough traditional country, you'll notice how mama always raises squirrelly kids who end up in trouble. In this case, her daughter's on Death Row with a mob outside the prison gates howling for her head, so I'm wondering if mama could've tried a little harder.

Still, you can't help but feel bad for Loretta and hope that she'll get a reprieve or some new evidence will turn up that will exonerate her. Maybe she shot her darlin' in self-defense, or there was a second gunman behind the grassy knoll next to the jukebox. No, Loretta is resigned to her fate. She can hear the warden approaching as she eats her last meal of fried chicken and grits (I know that's a stereotype but she started it). As they lead her away, Loretta tells us how a priest is giving her the last rites before telling her, "dyin's part of livin', y'know . . ." (gee, thanks for that note of comfort).

The song climaxes with Loretta being strapped into the electric chair to wait for the juice to flow. She can still hear her mama cry, it being "the last voice I hear on earth." The banging music drops down to just a hymn-like organ as Loretta softly sings "Amazing Grace" before fading into silence.

Why It's Depressing

What makes "Women's Prison" so ungodly morbid for me is the image of a demure Loretta Lynn being hit with 3,000 volts. It really is shocking to listen to, no pun intended, and there's something very disturbing about the way Loretta sings "Amazing Grace" under her breath while that nervous organ hums behind her, sounding like a harmonium played by a suicidal Shaker. Musically, "Women's Prison" is more roots-rock than country, resembling a garage band rehearsing with their death-obsessed grandmother. White's production work is very lo-fi and primal, as if they recorded it in Loretta's basement next to the canned peaches and Patsy Cline memorabilia. The amazing thing about "Women's Prison" is how archaic it is. I haven't heard a song like it since the Band covered Lefty Frizzell's "Long Black Veil," and that was a long time ago. Though prisons still show up plenty in country music, songs about convicts awaiting execution have pretty much disappeared and you never hear them sung by a woman. Since Loretta wrote the song, I'm trying to imagine what it must've sounded like before White got his alt-rock hands on it. I can hear it being done in a Nashville studio with a steel guitar driving the whole thing and a fiddle adding accents. It would still be depressing but not as much as the rattletrap version on *Van Lear Rose*.

Perfect Storms

Seasons in the Sun

Performed by Terry Jacks
Released 1974 (No. 1 in the UK and the US)
Original French lyrics and music by Jacques Brel
English translation by Rod McKuen

IN THE fetid world of Perfect Storm depressing songs, death reigns supreme. While countless songs have addressed death over the centuries, very few of them can be considered Perfect Storms. On the other hand, you cannot write a Perfect Storm without having some reference to death in the lyrics, along with an unquenchable desire to share it with the rest of the world. There, then, is the formula: mortality plus misguided passion.

In the 1970s, Canadian singer Terry Jacks and his then wife Susan Pesklevits made up the musical duo the Poppy Family, a sort of Great White North married version of the more-talented Carpenters. They scored a number-two hit in 1970 in the US with their song "Which Way You Goin', Billy?" engineered in such a gauzy rococo fashion that you'd think their moniker derived from the opium they were smoking when they recorded it. Three years later, the couple divorced and Jacks pursued a solo career. A competent producer, he was asked to help supervise a Beach Boys session (sans Brian Wilson) where he persuaded them to record a song he'd heard years earlier from the Kingston Trio entitled "Seasons in the Sun." The resulting track was deemed too depressing, though, and the group refused to release it. Undaunted, Jacks decided to record it himself. The rest is Perfect Storm history.

"Seasons in the Sun" tormented a whole generation of AM radio listeners in 1974, and even today the song has not lost its power to fold, spindle, and mutilate the human spirit. It's sung from the point of view of a terminally ill man on his deathbed bidding his farewells and, as we all know, anything a person utters while he's dying sounds a lot more profound than it would be otherwise (i.e., "where's the goddamned remote—AACK! *Uhhhnnnnng*..."). In the case of "Seasons in the Sun," the dying man gets to have his final words incorporated into a pop tune that went on to sell six million copies worldwide, thereby spreading musical depression globally.

I must emphasize that none of this is the fault of the song's original composer, the late, great Jacques Brel, who remains one of music's most innovative artists. Born in 1929 in Belgium, he found fame in Paris cabarets and theaters as a singer/entertainer who mesmerized audiences with his huge voice and charismatic stage presence. What made Brel unique was that he sang all his own material, and he just happened to be a brilliant songwriter who was way ahead of his time. An adequate if unexceptional music composer, Brel's gift was in his lyrics, and he cheekily composed scores of songs about lust, infidelity, religion, and hypocrisy, as well as aching love ballads. (His picaresque song "Amsterdam" should be taught in colleges.) A charming man who was lionized in Europe, Brel died of cancer in 1978.

One of Brel's songs was a melancholy composition entitled "Le Moribond," which he recorded in 1962. Sentimental yet harmless, "Le Moribond" is not one of Brel's better works, though its original final stanza is rather funny. As Brel sang almost exclusively in French, it took hack poet/songwriter Rod McKuen to translate "Le Moribond" into English. McKuen is the original Mr. Sensitive and he unfortunately bowdlerized the lyrics, stripping much of Brel's mischief to replace it with mawkish rhymes. He renamed it "Seasons in the Sun" and the bland folk group the Kingston Trio recorded the first English version of the song in 1963. Bad on every level (they played it way too fast), the record sold dismally yet it was this version that Terry Jacks heard and that somehow stayed with him over the years. After the Beach Boys scrapped the song, Jacks returned to his native Canada to record his own version of "Seasons in the Sun." He seemed determined to get rich by depressing the hell out of everyone. He even had the key changes ready.

The Song

The only good moment in "Seasons in the Sun" is the boomy opening guitar lick, played by legendary rock pioneer Link Wray of "Rumble" fame. (What was he doing at this session?) Spooky and basso profundo, you expect to hear some kickass rockabilly burst forth but, alas, the music settles into a medium-tempo rock beat, carried along by a nervously choppy keyboard figure that resembles a giant woodpecker drilling a hole into an organ. "Good-bye to you," Jacks sings to a nameless trusted friend. The dying man recalls how they've known each other since they were "nine or ten," spending their youth climbing trees and learning how to read. Keep in mind this man's recollections have been filtered through the sentiment-sucking psyche of Rod McKuen, so it's quite possible there was some underage drinking and some prank phone calls, too, which fail to get mentioned. "Good-bye, my friend," Jacks continues, "it's hard to die." There are birds in the sky and hot chicks for his friend to enjoy, though, and he tells him to "think of me and I'll be there."

At this point, the novice listener starts enduring the song's infamous chorus. It's nothing less than one giant earworm, something that you cannot get out of your head, try as you might. "We had joy, we had fun . . ." Jacks sings, referring to all their youthful hijinks as ". . . seasons in the sun." But all those pastoral seasons are gone now, replaced by a series of exhausting key changes that Jacks employs repeatedly throughout the chorus; each one is like a mini BCM.

As Wray revisits his cool guitar riff, the dying man says good-bye to "papa" while apologizing for being such a "black sheep." Between that and all the joy and fun he's remembering, the narrator comes across as a former trust-fund kid who probably had his pot dealer's phone number programed into his speed dial. There's no telling how often his father had to bail him out of jail. Jacks sings how there was always "too much wine" and that he still cannot fathom how he "got along" the way he did. Once again, the malignant chorus, "we had joy, we had fun . . ." followed by more pedal-to-the-metal modulations.

In the last stanza, the man bids farewell to a girl named Michelle, who never existed in Jacques Brel's lyrics. The Kingston Trio's otherwise campy cover of "Seasons in the Sun" is interesting because it contains the original verses, albeit sanitized by McKuen. Brel has the man bidding adieu to his "trusted wife" Françoise, admitting he would've had a "lonely life" without her. He also reminds her, and us, about all the times she "cheated" on him with his best friend. It comes out of nowhere and it's great classic Brel humor that not even McKuen could whitewash. Astonishingly, Terry Jacks threw out the lyrics and replaced them with his own set of verses in order to "brighten the song up." His idea of brightening was to have the man give a weepy farewell to "Michelle," the girl who helped him "find the sun." Now he's dying and only wishes he could be with her among all the birds and spring flowers. Yeah, thanks, Terry. That's so much happier.

The song's earworm chorus returns at the very end, with Jacks jumping keys over and over like an Olympic hurdler. There are no less than four modulations before it finally fades (the track fades, anyway; the chorus will keep looping in your head for a few weeks).

Why It's Depressing

Why this song deserves Perfect Storm status is based on a number of factors. First, there's Link Wray not being allowed to cut loose. Then, there's all the McKuenesque rhymes like "die" and "sky," "air" and "everywhere," plus the decision to replace Françoise the philandering spouse with Michelle the sun guide. But what really drops the anchor is all the maudlin good-byes in "Seasons in the Sun." First the friend with no name gets a good-bye, then papa, then Michelle, all of them buttressed by that damned key-changing chorus, which hangs inside your cerebrum like Spanish moss. I can still remember when I was young and radio stations played this song every hour on the hour; it was the traffic report of pop singles.

Having lost a close friend to lymphoma, I know what the last words of the terminally ill sound like and they bear no resemblance to the sap-filled nostalgia that Rod McKuen somehow conjured up from the French lyrics. (More accurate English translations of Brel's songs were made by Mort Shuman and Eric Blau for their musical revue *Jacques Brel Is Alive and Well*.) The last dying person to sound this maudlin was Ali McGraw in *Love Story*. All the rest of us humans just mumble something unintelligible, then check out. I've no idea what's wrong with the guy, anyway. Did too much hard living pickle his liver or did he get ahold of some bad coke? If his father is outliving him, it must be pretty bad.

Suffice to say, "Seasons in the Sun" is at least two degrees separated from the original source, which means it isn't really a Jacques Brel song. He'd never change keys like that.

Total Eclipse of the Heart

Performed by Bonnie Tyler
Released 1983 (No. 1 in the UK and the US)
Written by Jim Steinman

EVERY now and then I get a little bit cranky 'bout a song that hangs with me like a malignant boil. Every now and then I get a little bit down when I have to listen to it twenty times in an hour. Every now and then I get a little bit tempted to throw myself in front of a bus. Every now and then I get a little bit injured when the bus grinds me into the pavement . . .

Don't worry, I haven't lost my mind. I'm simply rephrasing the numbskull lyrics to Bonnie Tyler's depressing 1984 hit "Total Eclipse of the Heart" to voice my dread at having to revisit this monstrous *gestalt* song. After twenty years, it still vanquishes the will of all those who dare turn around to gaze into its bright eyes. Though not the most depressing song ever written, "Total Eclipse of the Heart" is, hands down, the most demented and we can thank Jim Steinman for unleashing it upon us.

Even if no one gets offed in the lyrics, there's still more than enough death in "Total Eclipse" to make it a Perfect Storm, if only because it seems to have killed Bonnie Tyler's career. The Welsh singer was pretty big a few decades back, starting with her first hit single "It's a Heartache" in 1977. Her trademark was a raspy singing voice that sounded like she gargled with Ajax. After the success of "It's a Heartache," though, Tyler's follow-up singles didn't chart well and she went in search of a new collaborator to prepare her for the 1980s. She wound up partnering with Jim Steinman, the songwriter behind Meat Loaf's infamous *Bat Out Of Hell* album which has to date sold

30 million copies worldwide. His reputation as a composer of twisted pop anthems outfitted with hari kari lyrics somehow appealed to Tyler and she was eager to work with him. The result was the schizoid transatlantic chart topper "Total Eclipse of the Heart." If you cross Brian Wilson with Bram Stoker and add more voices in the head, you'd have this song.

The Song

The opening piano of "Total Eclipse" sounds the clarion call for all of Steinman's winged succubi to assemble. Bonnie Tyler, swathed in druid clothing while sandpapering her larynx, awaits the master's cue. He is hunched over a Steinway inside the darkened ballroom of a crumbling antebellum mansion (they're always antebellum), playing his Freddy-Kruger-at-rest intro while a raven perches on his shoulder. "Turn arrouuuuund," a boy soprano with shriveled genitalia sings with ethereal ease. This is Bonnie's cue: "Every now and then I get a little bit lonely . . ." As the music creeps along like a ghost with a hangover, we find out that "every now and then" Bonnie Tyler gets a little bit "lonely," a little bit "tired," a little bit "nervous" and a little bit "terrified." And let's not forget a little bit "restless," "helpless," and "angry." Basically, she's a little bit nuts. She's everything a guy would want in a woman. (Did you know she listens to the sound of her tears?)

This leads her to fall apart "every now and then," though I suspect it's more often than that. And why shouldn't she? She's been handed so many neurotic verses, she sounds like she's quoting the collected works of Sybil. The constant repetition of "every now and then I get a little bit . . ." goes beyond maddening and you wonder if Steinman's neurons were misfiring when he wrote the lyrics.

Eventually, someone bribes Steinman to get on with it and bring in a chorus. Bonnie Tyler ups her rasp, declaring "I need you now tonight! And I need you more than ever . . . !" That may be, but after hearing how angry, nervous, and terrified she gets "every now and then," the guy probably bolted like a gazelle. The more the song goes on, the more frenzied it gets. Tyler literally screams how "we're living in a powder keg" that's about to be ignited, howling with such conviction I suspect Steinman was dangling a live rat in front of her. When the histrionics subside, Tyler laments how there used to be light in her life "but now there's only love in the dark." It is, she sings with consummate weirdness, "a total eclipse of the heart."

Right when you think this song is over, the Rasputin Effect comes into play and resurrects it. An overblown instrumental passage that sounds like Steinman's scoring an oil tanker disaster pounds forth until Tyler begins reciting even more "every now and then . . ." mantras. Finally, she turns her voice into Angus Young's amplifier and shreds her way through the chorus again. A choir of voices (human optional) back her up as she makes her final futile wail about how "forever's gonna start tonight . . . !" The volcano crescendo ends after half the session musicians drop dead and Steinman's deranged piano carries the bodies away. "Total Eclipse" doesn't really end as much as become extinct. The fade alone lasts forty-five seconds, pushing the song's running time past the seven-minute mark.

Why It's Depressing

There are few songs, depressing and otherwise, as exhausting as "Total Eclipse." Listening to it is like an opera company bludgeoning you with copies of Anne Rice novels. The song is Steinman's "Ring Cycle" without the funny hats, a perverse attempt at neo-Romantic gothic bombast being sung by a woman trying to out-growl Kim Carnes. "Total Eclipse" begins creepy, turns disturbing, and ends up totally psychotic.

You're completely drained when it's over and desperately in need of a shower so you can rinse off the raven droppings.

Bonnie Tyler never repeated the success of "Total Eclipse of the Heart" ("Holding Out for a Hero" doesn't count) and her album sales languished. It's as if she sold her soul for a chance to live in the mad world of Jim Steinman just to see what it was like. Though she climbed a mountain with "Total Eclipse," it cursed her with a song that today is all but banned from Adult Contemporary radio. You're more likely to hear that the Beatles are reuniting than a station play "Total Eclipse of the Heart." Turn around, bright eyes. And look at the mess you left.

Honey

Performed by Bobby Goldsboro
Released 1968 (No. 2 in the UK, no. 1 in the US)
Written by Bobby Russell

I FIND myself in a quandary. How do you write about a man as nice, talented, wholesome, intelligent, and dedicated to children as Bobby Goldsboro when he's also the man who recorded one of the most molar-wrenching, eye-gouging, arsenic-gulping, artery-carving, impale-me-on-a-roasting-spit depressing songs ever written? The soppy death ballad "Honey," which involves a guy reminiscing about his deceased wife, is a ready candidate for Perfect Storm status as it has everything: maudlin lyrics, deadly earnest vocal delivery, sappy strings, and no discernible reason as to why it should exist other than to force listeners to dash their brains out with a ball peen hammer.

Goldsboro began his career in the early 1960s as a guitarist for the late, great Roy Orbison before finding success as a solo singer of easy listening pap that featured his vibrato-cursed voice. The general public, still afraid of the Rolling Stones, found both him and his white-as-yeast songs comforting; even their titles were cutesy: "See the Funny Little Clown," "Watching Scotty Grow," and the like. Then in 1968 at the height of the Tet offensive, Goldsboro released his cover of an appalling ballad entitled "Honey" and, for a brief time, Vietnam didn't seem quite so bad. The song was written by the late songwriter Bobby Russell who somehow got inducted into the Nashville Songwriters Hall of Fame for penning some of the worst hit songs ever, including "Little Green Apples" (another Goldsboro hit) and the depressingly awful "The Night the Lights Went Out in Georgia" which his then wife Vicki Lawrence recorded. Karaoke machines are known to self-destruct if forced to play it, but it cannot hold a bipolar candle to "Honey," a number-one hit in 1968 and one of the biggest-selling singles of all time, naturally. (I've given up on adverbs invoking surprise.) There's a conspiracy theory in there somewhere that involves aliens with pods because no rational human can possibly listen to "Honey" without wanting to pull a double Van Gogh and hack off their own ears.

I looked for any viable excuse not to include "Honey" in this book other than maybe it was over-qualified. I couldn't think of any, so I loaded up on Scotch and forced myself to revisit the maudlin death ditty that is "Honey." I began with remakes, my theory being they wouldn't be as bad and then I'd be prepared when I finally came face-to-face with the Beast, that being Goldsboro's version. Pianist Floyd Cramer's instrumental muzak rendition reacquainted me with the phrase-heavy melody of "Honey," which (music theory joke approaching) sounds like 300 appoggiaturas standing in the unemployment line. I moved on to smooth country baritone Eddy Arnold's cover. His grandfatherly vocals over a waft of Nashville strings were blissfully soporific and I fell asleep before hearing anything disturbing. Roger Whittaker? I have no idea because five seconds into his version, I heard an oboe and sprained my wrist shutting it off.

I decided I was as ready as I'd ever be.

The Song

Over a bed of strings, Goldsboro begins with a scene right out of a Hallmark Hall of Fame movie: a man standing in his backyard and studying a large tree, commenting to someone on how much it's grown. But at one time "Friend . . . it wasn't big." The tree began as just a twig that was planted by his late wife

Honey, who is patronizingly described as "kinda dumb and kinda smart." (Since she's dead, she wouldn't be offended.)

We get to hear a lot about who Honey was, like how she once slipped on some ice and fell, almost injuring herself. "I laughed 'til I cried," Goldsboro tells us. (That's nice. How about helping her up, you prick?) She used to cry herself, by the way, after watching some "sad and silly late late show," probably the *Tonight Show* with special guest Bobby Goldsboro doing this freaking song. "I surprised her with a puppy," he continues, one that made him stay up all night, too. This lyric serves absolutely no narrative purpose other than to work a puppy into the song.

Goldsboro sings in the chorus about missing Honey, adding how he'd love to be with her if only he could. Since this was before restraining orders came into vogue, we must assume he cannot be with Honey because she died. We are briefly tricked when the next verse tells us how she crashed the car and subsequently was sad, but this is not a teenage car crash song. She wasn't hurt, just afraid that he'd be upset, but he really wasn't. After all, she can't help it. She's stupid and clumsy, remember? Then everything changes one day.

Goldsboro continues plaintively, singing of coming home to find her crying, his vibrato so pronounced you could go surfing in it. Now comes the depression barrage, being the arrival of spring, filled with blooming flowers and singing robins. This is when Honey goes away. "One day when I wasn't home," Goldsboro sings, "the angels came." Honey, ill from some terminal disease, expires alone in the house. Her demise is both tragic and odd. If she was dying, "Where were you?!" you want to scream. Why would you not be home while your wife is on her deathbed? But he's not paying attention, for his life is now just an empty stage "where Honey played." He wakes up at night calling out her name while "a small cloud cries" down on a flowerbed that Honey once planted.

Why It's Depressing

"Honey" is by far the wordiest depressing song ever written, crammed full of blooming flowers, puffy clouds, angels, singing robins, planted trees, and the puppy. It's as if Bobby Russell loaded up on as many cloying images as he could find so there'd be no excuse for people not to wail like coyotes. But it's Goldsboro's reedy tenor and wide-eyed delivery that crank up the gooey melodrama that infests this song like the bubonic plague. More than thirty-five years after its release, it remains one of the most depressing songs ever conceived.

If any uninitiated readers plan on listening to "Honey" just for yuks, please don't. But if you must, then I strongly urge you to drink heavily and then bail from it after Honey wrecks the car. You'll have already heard about the puppy, the planted tree, her young heart, the snow in the yard, their joyous times together, and the implication that Honey is dead. After that, turn the goddamn song off and run like a cheetah because if you stay till the end, you'll get hit with spring, angels, Honey's name being called out, and clouds crying on flowerbeds. You won't make it out with your senses intact; trust me, it is that bad. After all, "Honey" is a Perfect Storm.

The Shortest Story

Performed by Harry Chapin
Released 1976
Words and Music by Harry Chapin

BEFORE HIS death at age thirty-eight in a traffic accident in 1981, the singer-songwriter Harry Chapin was an unstinting champion of the oppressed, and devoted much of his life to combating poverty and world hunger. He raised millions of dollars for charity playing benefit concerts while giving away his own money and tirelessly lobbying Congress for federal aid. Never a big seller and dismissed by critics, Chapin none the less had a loyal following of fans who were attracted to his sincerity and charming manner. In short, Harry Chapin was a decent human being who just happened to write one of the most horribly depressing songs in the history of pop music.

Harry Chapin was born in 1942 in Long Island, New York, and formed a folk group with his brothers Tom and Steve that performed in Greenwich Village during the early 1960s. He later worked in film production and even received an Oscar nomination for his 1969 boxing documentary *Legendary Champions*. He continued to write and perform his narrative songs in clubs, landing a recording contract in 1971 when the labels were signing singer-songwriters. His long and slightly fatuous ballad "Taxi" became a staple of FM radio (likely because of its lyric ". . . takin' tips and gettin' stoned") and he scored a number-one hit in 1974 with the sentimental "Cat's in the Cradle." Prolific and earnest to a fault, Chapin was never a great tunesmith and tended to write songs with on-the-nose lyrics outfitted with clunky rhymes. Though he could be funny in concert, Chapin sometimes took himself a little too seriously, especially in his charity work. No one doubted his commitment and generosity, but many a hapless person found themselves cornered by Chapin as he harangued them about global economics, reeling reams of statistics off the top of his head while the listener's eyes glazed over. It is exactly this kind of misguided didacticism that infects his song "The Shortest Story."

A studio track, which closes out his 1976 concert album *Greatest Stories Live*, "The Shortest Story" is about—are you ready for this?—an infant who dies of malnutrition. I'm not kidding. In fact, the song is sung from the viewpoint of an infant who dies of malnutrition. This is so not a good idea.

The Song

The first time you hear "The Shortest Story," you know you're in trouble just from the opening alone: A twelve-string guitar and a tubular bell ring out a single note in unison. Like the oboe, tubular bells do not belong within a hunter's mile of any studio where a song is being produced unless it's the theme to a movie about demonic possession. No percussion device portends death better than a set of tubular bells; they're the banshee of musical instruments. Finally Chapin is heard. "I am born today," he sings mournfully. With no doctor or midwife around, the infant's birth mother must slap the child "and I draw a breath and cry . . ." He sees clouds above him, indicating that he was likely born outside in a field, his family living in squalor in Biafra, Bangladesh, the Sudan, Ethiopia, anyplace there's poor farmland, political chaos, and no rainfall. "I am glad to be alive," Chapin adds.

A string quartet creeps in, depressing the proceedings even more (some sick engineer over-miked the cello). It is a week later and the infant can "taste the hunger and I cry . . ." Mama, who has her other two children clinging to her, is so malnourished she cannot nurse. All around him are the sounds of children crying from lack of food. "Someone weeps," Chapin sings.

In case you're wondering, week-old infants are not normally this articulate, except in those cutesy *Look Who's Talking* movies where babies come into the world with their own voiceovers and a team of joke writers. Call me superficial, but I prefer those kind of babies. The one in Chapin's song has been handed a raw deal, but being so tiny and undeveloped, he cannot raise a revolt or even steal a neighbor's chicken. This obviously was Chapin's point but there are better ways to express it. One alternative is . . . anything else except sing this song.

Twenty days later, the infant lies neglected. Too weak to cry, he stares up at a bird that "crawls across the sky" (birds that crawl?). Finally, Chapin brings it home with guillotine-like efficiency as the infant asks rhetorically why is "there nothing now to do but DIE!" The tubular bell returns with a clang, chiming three times over the desolate sound of rushing wind. The only thing that saves "The Shortest Story" from being a number-one Perfect Storm is the accuracy of the title. The song is mercifully brief; any longer and you'd be gnawing your leg off.

Why It's Depressing

I know, I'm being harsh about a song written by a man who cannot defend himself but, come on, does anybody really want to listen to something like this? Did die-hard Chapin fans blissfully hold up lit Zippo lighters whenever he broke into "The Shortest Story" during his shows? Who among us could sit through such a horrid song and not feel like someone is peeling the skin off our skulls with the key to a sardine can?

Chapin's obsession with eliminating world hunger made him an effective ambassador and spokesperson for the disenfranchised, but it often turned his muse into an agitprop fanatic whose ancestors bombed Haymarket Square. He composed more than a few protest songs meant to instill "awareness" of various social problems, but "The Shortest Story" goes so far overboard, it takes the ship with it. We're all very aware of the horrors of famine. We've read the "Sponsor a child" ads in newspapers, seen Sally Struthers in the African village yammering on about dysentery, watched the Live Aid concert, and got sick of "We Are the World." Awareness we have. Getting slammed over the head with this suicide-inducing tubular-bell-ringing folkie nightmare is something we don't need. "The Shortest Story" is the equivalent of someone dumping fifty tons of raw nuclear waste in the middle of a park to demonstrate how bad it is to litter.

If I sound obsessive (read: disturbed) about "The Shortest Story," I have reason to be: I had to play it once for a Christmas program (you read that right). It was 1981 and I was still in college. A friend of mine named George asked if I'd play guitar to accompany him on a song he wanted to sing at his church.

"What song are you going to do?" I asked.

"It's called 'The Shortest Story,'" he said. "It's by Harry Chapin."

I knew some of Chapin's songs but couldn't recall that one. I asked George to play it for me so I could figure out the chords. He put it on and I listened to it, tubular bells and all. After my delirium wore off, I looked at George in total bewilderment. "You wanna sing that song for a Christmas program?"

"I want people to know that there are others less fortunate than us," he said. "The holidays are about giving."

I could've begged out of it. I could've played sick. I could've pretended I sprained my hand, but for reasons I still don't understand, I consented to accompany George on his mission to sing "The Shortest Story" to help celebrate Christmas.

The following Sunday, I arrived at a Lutheran church near the campus and sat in a pew with George and his girlfriend, Lisa. Two young women were on the altar cheerily singing Christmas carols while strumming out-of-tune classical guitars. A third played a flute in a manner that can only be described as "primitive." It was all very warm and cheerful, and I silently wished they'd break into a John Coltrane number and jam all morning. But, alas, our time came and the minister introduced us to the congregation. George and I went up to the altar and I sat down with my acoustic, sweating cannonballs. "What am I doing here?" I asked myself.

"Good morning," George greeted them. "Though we're all looking forward to Christmas, we should remember that there are those less fortunate than us . . ." (as he introduced the song, the parishioners gazed back with complete trust; I looked around and mentally noted the fire exits) ". . . and it's called 'The Shortest Story.' "

George nodded to me, closed his eyes, and we began. "I am born today," he sang.

To this day, I will not forget the sight of 200 Lutherans slowly twisting their faces into expressions of utter horror while George and I performed this African famine ditty. By the time we got to the line about the mother vainly squeezing her breast, every pew featured a dozen people who resembled Edvard Munch's *The Scream*. I bent my head into the lowest vulture crouch I could adopt and stared at my shoes. Though "The Shortest Story" is a short song, the whole experience felt longer than a Proust novel. After an eternity, we arrived at the end and George punctuated the final verse, ". . . nothing left to do but DIE!" It was over.

The applause, I have to say, was not deafening. There was a slight pause. Then another. Then another. Finally, some tepid clapping was heard. It was the most relieved applause I've ever heard; they were clapping because it was over.

I never accompanied George again.

I bear Chapin's memory no ill will; he was passionate about fighting world hunger and put his money and efforts where his mouth was. I'm sure he's in the heavens right now serenading numerous winged spirits with "Taxi" and "Cat's in the Cradle" while St. Peter keeps requesting "30,000 Pounds of Bananas" because it makes him laugh. But there's no way any cloud-walking agents of the Lord ever allow him to sing "The Shortest Story." I should know; I was there.

The Christmas Shoes

Performed by Newsong
Released 2000 (No. 1 on Adult Contemporary charts in the US)
Words and Music by Leonard Ahlstrom and Eddie Carswell

SOMETIMES the best intentions are the catalyst that triggers the fission bomb. This is why the most diabolically depressing songs began as a righteous effort at striking an emotional chord with the masses while their creators are clueless as to the horror they've created. Think Dr. Frankenstein gazing down at his monster and seeing Adonis. Think Kurt Cobain looking at Courtney Love and seeing Courtney Cox. Think a Christian group writing a song about a boy buying a pair of shoes for his dying mother and thinking it's spiritually uplifting. Think again.

I set out to find the most depressing song ever written and I'm certain I found it. It makes Bobby Goldsboro's "Honey" sound like The Red Hot Chili Peppers. It's more depressing than Jim Morrison puking in front of a naked Indian in a Paris hotel room. It's more depressing than Trent Reznor and Marilyn Manson singing a duet of "Danny Boy" while jamming syringes into each other's eyes. It's more depressing than the Cure's entire career. It's more depressing than that mind-fucking Harry Chapin malnutrition song. It's the most depressing song ever written because it's long, criminally insufferable, and, worst of all, Christmas themed, which means we will always hear it during the Yuletide season year after year.

It's "The Christmas Shoes."

I was blissfully unaware of "The Christmas Shoes" until someone told me about a song she always heard in department stores during the Christmas holidays, floating down from overhead along with Amy Grant, Burl Ives, and Christy Lane. It's about a little boy buying a pair of shoes for his dying mother, she said, and it's really depressing. *Hmm*, I thought, *little boy, dying mother, a gift of shoes . . . Sounds like a bad idea to me. I'm there!*

Finding "The Christmas Shoes" was easy. Listening to it was not. After just one spin, I went into the sort of shock normally associated with survivors of asteroid collisions. I couldn't quite comprehend what I'd just heard. It was such a misfire it could sink an aircraft carrier. Worse yet, the thought of this song being played constantly around the holiday season was just too terrifying for me to comprehend. After much Googled research, I uncovered a saga so twisted it resembled a Hitchcock movie by way of the Book of Revelations.

"The Christmas Shoes" is the work of the contemporary Christian group Newsong. They've recorded over thirteen albums and are very popular in the faith-based Christian market. In 1999, group leader Eddie Carswell found a story that was circulating around the Internet entitled "The Golden Christmas Slippers." An anonymous author wrote a first-person account of something he allegedly witnessed at a Target shopping center in Houston (I used to live in Houston and, yes, there is a Target there). Though nobody knows who wrote it, most people still insist it's true.

In "The Golden Christmas Slippers," the writer tells of wearily standing in a long line waiting to check out. It is five days before Christmas and he's feeling burned-out from all the stress of shopping and obligatory gift giving. The following is supposedly what transpired next:

> In front of me were two small children—a boy of
> about ten and a younger girl about five. The boy wore a
> ragged coat. Enormously large, tattered tennis shoes
> jutted far out in front of his much-too-short jeans. He

clutched several crumpled dollar bills in his grimy hands. The girl's clothing resembled her brother's. Her head was a matted mass of curly hair. Reminders of an evening meal showed on her small face. She carried a beautiful pair of shiny, gold house slippers. As the Christmas music sounded in the store's stereo system, the girl hummed along off-key but happily.

When we finally approached the checkout register, the girl carefully placed the shoes on the counter. She treated them as though they were a treasure. The clerk rang up the bill. "That will be $6.09," she said. The boy laid his crumpled dollars atop the stand while he searched his pockets. He finally came up with $3.12.

"I guess we will have to put them back," he bravely said. "We will come back some other time, maybe tomorrow."

With that statement, a soft sob broke from the little girl. "But Jesus would have loved these shoes," she cried.

"Well, we'll go home and work some more. Don't cry. We'll come back," he said.

Quickly I handed $3.00 to the cashier. These children had waited in line for a long time. And, after all, it was Christmas. Suddenly a pair of arms came around me and a small voice said, "Thank you, sir."

"What did you mean when you said Jesus would like the shoes?" I asked.

The small boy answered, "Our mommy is sick and going to heaven. Daddy said she might go before Christmas to be with Jesus."

The girl spoke: "My Sunday school teacher said the streets in Heaven are shiny gold, just like these shoes. Won't mommy be beautiful walking on those streets to match these shoes?"

My eyes flooded as I looked into her tear-streaked face. "Yes," I answered, "I am sure she will." Silently I thanked God for using these children to remind me of the true spirit of giving.

I know I'll be branded a heartless heretic but if any of you actually believe this story, I have wonderful tales of reincarnated rabbits and Jersey devils to regale you with. Never mind his Dickensian clothing, how many ten-year-old boys say declarative sentences like, "We will have to put them back. We will come back some other time, maybe tomorrow." How about a five-year-old saying, "The streets in Heaven are shiny gold, just like these shoes. Won't mommy be beautiful walking on those streets to match these shoes?" I can tell right now who wrote this story: somebody who's never been around a ten- and a five-year-old.

Whether or not Eddie Carswell believed the story is a moot point. He felt compelled to adapt "The Golden Christmas Slippers" into a song, one for which he wouldn't have to share any royalties with the author. He and bandmate Leonard Ahlstrom put together a ballad they entitled simply "The Christmas Shoes" and included it on their 2000 CD release *Sheltering Tree*. The song was first played as a single on a Christian radio station in St. Louis and, supposedly, it was swamped with calls. "The Christmas Shoes" eventually broke into the mainstream market and topped the Adult Contemporary charts. (I've no idea what "Adult Contemporary" signifies other than it's contemporary music purchased by adults.)

Following the mainstream success of the song, Newsong switched labels and rereleased it in 2001 as the title cut on their Christmas holiday album *The Christmas Shoes*. It, too, was a hit. From here on, the song became a Perfect Storm assault weapon. First, Nashville author Donna Van Liere adapted it into a novella of the same name and it became a *New York Times* best-seller. Then Hollywood came a-callin' and CBS produced a two-hour-long TV movie based on a book that was based on a song that was based on a story written by a guy who fibs a lot. *The Christmas Shoes,* starring Rob Lowe, premiered on December 21, 2001 and drew 17 million viewers. It's been re-aired every December since. "The Christmas Shoes" had been a phenomenon and I'd slept through the entire thing.

The Song

"The Christmas Shoes" begins in prototypical AC ballad form, with processed MIDI piano and nylon-string guitar playing a cloying intro until vocalist Billy Goodwin begins. "It was almost Christmas time," he sings, telling of standing in line at a department store to check out and finding it hard to get into the Christmas spirit. From here, "The Christmas Shoes" follows the Internet story almost exactly, the exception being there's a lone boy in line ahead of him. Goodwin points out how dirty the boy is and that his clothes were old and worn. The unkempt lad has a pair of shoes in his hands and when he finally reaches the cashier, the man overhears the boy's sad tale of woe, how his daddy says there's not much time left for Mommy. All he wants is to bring the shoes to her so she can look beautiful "if Mama meets Jesus tonight." (Who knew the Messiah was such a stickler for footwear?)

The little boy dumps a hoard of pennies (more theatrical than crumpled bills) and the cashier counts them. Naturally, there's not enough and the kid turns to the man behind him, explaining how Mama always did without just to make "Christmas good at our house." Now she's on her deathbed and all he wants is to buy her the shoes for her last Christmas. As his Grinch façade melts, the man hands the boy some money and watches his cherubic face light up. "Mama's gonna look great," the child tells him (she'd better or else Jesus is going to be very, very angry). The song moves into a bridge as the man declares how he's "caught a glimpse of Heaven's love." See, it was God who sent this little boy to him for the sole purpose of showing him the meaning of Christmas. Meanwhile the dirty, ragged-looking boy runs off alone and unaccompanied, something this moron fails to notice since he's too busy congratulating himself for learning to enjoy Christmas again.

The chorus returns and damned if it's not a choir of children's voices singing, "Sir, I want to buy these shoes for my mama, please . . ." There's not enough insulin in the world to combat this lethal dose of confection that drips like snow slush from a dead birch tree. I heaved so hard, my shoes came up.

Why It's Depressing

Though I've endured the most violent nihilistic musical crud ever conceived, none of it holds a candle to the Krakatoa-sized cataclysm that is "The Christmas Shoes." What throws me into the volcano about both the song and the apocryphal story that inspired it is their insufferable smugness and ludicrous storytelling. What father sends his little boy to a department store by himself in threadbare clothing to buy a pair of shoes when Mom's about to shuffle off any minute? Is the guy a crack addict? Does he have a drug lab going in the kitchen? What's this about, anyway? Meanwhile, the narrator has to be the most clueless dip this side of Inspector Clousseau. If you were standing in a checkout line and a filthy child resembling Oliver Twist was in front of you with no adult accompanying him, wouldn't you, oh I don't know, NOTIFY SECURITY? Not this genius. He just tosses the kid a few bucks and then thanks God for showing him "a sign of Heaven's love." This was Heaven's great idea? Afflict a child's mother with a terminal disease, then send him to Target by himself to buy her a pair of shoes without enough money for the sole purpose of making some self-righteous jerk feel good about himself? Couldn't he at least offer the kid a ride?

The fact that "The Christmas Shoes" is a well-loved song

doesn't alter my conclusion that it's depressing manipulative swill that frankly isn't very original. The lyrics simply copy a fraudulent story that itself is a pale imitation of the classic Christmas story "The Littlest Angel" by Charles Tazewell. A sublime and beautiful tale, "The Littlest Angel" is so moving it would make rocks weep and offers a much more powerful message of giving than a thousand tales of Yuletide Florsheims. This holiday season, please read "The Littlest Angel" aloud to your children and forget you ever heard the condescending, depressing bilge of "The Christmas Shoes."

I hate this song. Merry Christmas to all and to all a good night.

~~Afterword~~
Honorable Mentions, Plus the Future

AFTER LISTENING to thousands of sad, downbeat, tragic, melancholy, gloomy, heartrending, distressing, and moody songs, I naturally had to exclude many worthy contenders from my ultimate list of fifty-two titles. No doubt the people responsible for them aren't very broken up about this, but then again I must give credit where credit is due.

Dickey Lee's disturbing 1962 weeper "Patches" definitely deserves mention as it'll wipe out anybody on first listen. The song tells of Patches, a poor girl from the wrong side of the tracks in love with a boy from a respectable family. He wants to marry her but his parents forbid it. Instead of defying them, he simply stops seeing her and never explains why. Heartbroken, Patches drowns herself in the river and the guilt-stricken boy decides to join her. "Patches, I'm coming to you," he declares, standing on the riverbank with rocks stuffed in his pockets. It took the Kennedy assassination the following year to get people's minds off of it.

Another notable tune that almost made the cut is the unsettling death-by-hypothermia ballad "Wildfire," which hit No. 3 in the US in 1975. This Michael Martin Murphy song is about a girl who freezes to death while searching for her lost pony Wildfire during a blizzard. "She ran calling, 'Wiiiiiild-fire!,'" Murphy wails during the depressing chorus. At the end, the frozen girl and Wildfire are coming to him so they can all ride away together. I still bolt from the room anytime this freaking horse-sicle song turns up on muzak.

For contemporary rock tunes, Simple Plan's whiny "Perfect" from 2002 was a runner-up, as it's the most depressing song I've ever heard that expresses the rage of a teenager upset about being told to take out the garbage. "Did I grow up according to plan?" he bitches to Dad in a snippy tone. Well, if the plan is to end up living in a trailer park with Trish the checkout girl from Wal-Mart, then, yeah, his future's set.

Likewise, Nashville delivered a dandy artery-choker in 2000 from country artist John Michael Montgomery with his murder-suicide song "The Little Girl." This bewildering "inspirational" song about a young girl being raised by two dysfunctional infidels ("Daddy drank . . . Mama did drugs") culminates with her hiding behind the couch while her enraged father blows her stoned mother away, then kills himself. The song's upbeat ending in which a loving, churchgoing couple adopt the little girl does nothing to offset all the Green Acres histrionics that precede it.

The corporatization of the music industry coupled with the current chart success of hip-hop and featherweight pop has stifled the creation of more memorable depressing songs. With the emphasis on vapid, upbeat material, fewer performers are attempting to record emotionally charged songs that wind up a prong-chomping mess. What depressing song fans wouldn't give to hear, say, Norah Jones throw herself into a remake of Gilbert O'Sullivan's suicidal "Alone Again (Naturally)." As Ms. Jones sings like Janis Ian following electro-shock therapy, her sibilant voice would be perfect for O'Sullivan's sing-along ode to offing himself. That would truly be depressing. Certainly, we have the possibility that an up-and-coming pop diva will be discovered who can unleash a grim über-ballad of Nagasaki proportions, but how long is *American Idol* going to be on the air?

The future of depressing music seems to lie in one-man musical groups outfitted with non sequitur names. Nine Inch Nails is Trent Reznor, Badly Drawn Boy is Damon Gough, and Bright Eyes is Conor Oberst, a gifted if seemingly self-important young singer-songwriter from Omaha, Nebraska. There's something about being isolated in a studio with nothing but an acoustic guitar, drum machine, Fender bass, vintage 1980s analog synth, and twenty-eight half-empty coffee cups that enables all these neo-bohemians to create memorably depressing music that appeals to people who spend the day slamming their hands in car doors. Bright Eyes' Oberst in particular looks to be carrying the gloom torch quite eagerly. His mopey songs capture the spirit of introspective predecessors like Elliot Smith and Ron Sexsmith, the former a suicide, the latter the guy who depressed the shit out of me at Largo in LA several years back (and he only played one song). One Bright Eyes tune in particular reared its miserable head to me recently: "No Lies, Just Love," about a suicidal teenager. Slow to the point of inert, the song features Oberst singing about procuring a bottle of pills on a cold March day for the sole purpose of killing himself. His ennui appears to be seasonal as the feeling lifts somewhat one month later when spring arrives. Eventually, he decides to live in order to be a doting uncle to his brother's new baby. The music is very DIY, the emotions sincere, the lyrics unambiguous. It is also the most depressing song I've heard so far from Generation Y.

Go forth, young man, and conquer.

The Final
Countdown

From 52 to 1 . . .

52. "Same Old Lang Syne"—Dan Fogelberg
51. "Artificial Flowers"—Bobby Darin
50. "Love Will Tear Us Apart"—Joy Division
49. "Teen Angel"—Mark Dinning
48. "Landslide"—Smashing Pumpkins
47. "Lucky Man"—Emerson Lake & Palmer
46. "Captain Jack"—Billy Joel
45. "Indiana Wants Me"—R. Dean Taylor
44. "Sylvia's Mother"—Dr. Hook and the Medicine Show
43. "The Wreck of the Edmund Fitzgerald"—Gordon Lightfoot
42. "In the Year 2525 (Exordium And Terminus)"—Zager and Evans
41. "Send in the Clowns"—Everybody
40. "Without You"—Mariah Carey
39. "It Must Be Him"—Vicki Carr
38. "Alone Again (Naturally)"—Gilbert O'Sullivan
37. "Let Her Cry"—Hootie and the Blowfish
36. "At Seventeen"—Janis Ian
35. "Beth"—Kiss
34. "Good-bye to Love"—The Carpenters
33. "Don't Cry Out Loud"—Melissa Manchester
32. "Mandy"—Barry Manilow
31. "Last Kiss"—J. Frank Wilson and the Cavaliers
30. "The End"—The Doors
29. "I Will Always Love You"—Whitney Houston
28. "Round Here"—Counting Crows
27. "MacArthur Park"—Richard Harris
26. "In the Air Tonight"—Phil Collins
25. "Sam Stone"—John Prine
24. "My Immortal"—Evanescence

23. "You Don't Bring Me Flowers"—Neil Diamond and Barbra Streisand
22. "The River"—Bruce Springsteen
21. "Tell Laura I Love Her"—Ray Peterson
20. "All By Myself"—Celine Dion
19. "Women's Prison"—Loretta Lynn
18. "Prayers for Rain"—The Cure
17. "The Freshmen"—The Verve Pipe
16. "The Rose"—Bette Midler
15. "Maggie's Dream"—Don Williams
14. "Comfortably Numb"—Pink Floyd
13. "Brick"—Ben Folds Five
12. "Ruby, Don't Take Your Love to Town"—Kenny Rogers and the First Edition
11. "One"—Metallica
10. "People Who Died"—The Jim Carroll Band
9. "Sister Morphine"—Marianne Faithfull
8. "Hurt"—Nine Inch Nails
7. "Strange Fruit"—Billie Holiday
6. "DOA"—Bloodrock
5. "Seasons in the Sun"—Terry Jacks
4. "Total Eclipse of the Heart"—Bonnie Tyler
3. "Honey"—Bobby Goldsboro
2. "The Shortest Story"—Harry Chapin
1. "The Christmas Shoes"—Newsong

Acknowledgments

The author would like to thank the following people for their help and support:

Denise Bellingham, William Bellingham, Erin Hayes, Kara Hayes.

Jeanne and Gunnard Reynolds and family.

Emily Gould and Rachelle Nashner at Hyperion.

John and Christy Michaels, and Don Welty.

Special thanks to Stacey Earley for her appropriately gloomy illustrations.

Dedicated to serotonin-challenged songwriters everywhere. You know who you are and I know where you live.

Credits

"Tell Laura I Love Her," 1960: Words and music, Jeff Barry/Ben Raleigh; Copyright: EMI Music Publishing, Ltd.

"Teen Angel," 1960: Words and music, Jean Surrey/Red Surrey; Copyright: Acuff-Rose Music, Ltd.

"Last Kiss," 1964: Words and music, Wayne Cochran; Copyright: Lark Music, Ltd.

"Good-bye to Love," 1972: Words and music, Richard Carpenter and John Bettis; Copyright: Render Music (London), Ltd.

"At Seventeen," 1975: Words and music, Janis Ian; Copyright: EMI Music Publishing, Ltd.

"My Immortal," 2004: Words and music, Amy Lee, Ben Moody, and David Hodges; Copyright: EMI Music Publishing, Ltd.

"It Must Be Him," 1967: Words and music, Gilbert Becaud, Mack David, Maurice Vidalin; Copyright: Sacem/David Mack Music Publ. Co./Sparta Florida Music Group, Ltd.

"One," 1989: Words and music, James Hetfield, Lars Ulrich; Copyright: Universal Music Publishing, Ltd.

"Round Here," 1994: Words and music, Adam Duritz, David Bryson, Dave Janusko, Dan Jewett, and Chris Roldan; Copyright: EMI Music Publishing, Ltd.

"Lucky Man," 1971: Words and music, Greg Lake; Copyright: EMI Music Publishing, Ltd.

"Beth," 1976: Words and music, Peter Criss, Stan Penridge, Bob Ezrin. Copyright: Hori Productions America, Inc. admin. by PolyGram International Publishing, Inc.

"MacArthur Park," 1968: Words and music, Jimmy Webb; Copyright: Universal Music Publishing, Ltd.

"Don't Cry Out Loud," 1978: Words and music, Peter Allen and Carol Bayer Sager; Copyright: Rendar Music (London), Ltd./Warner/Chappell

"In the Year 2525," 1969: Words and music, Richard Evans; Copyright: Chelsea Music Publishing, Ltd.

"Same Old Lang Syne," 1981: Words and music, Dan Fogelberg; Copyright: EMI Music Publishing, Ltd.

"The Rose," 1980: Words and music, Amanda McBroom; Copyright: Warner Chappell North America

"Mandy," 1974: Words and music, Scott English and Richard Kerr; Copyright: Chappell-Morris, Ltd./EMI Music Publishing, Ltd.

"Captain Jack," 1974: Words and music, Billy Joel; Copyright: EMI Music Publishing, Ltd.

"Let Her Cry," 1994: Words and music, Mark Bryan, Dean Felber, Darius Rucker, and Jim Sonefeld; Copyright: EMI Music Publishing, Ltd.

"Sam Stone," 1972: Words and music, John Prine; Copyright: Warner Chappell North America

"Love Will Tear Us Apart," 1980: Words and music, Ian Curtis, Peter Hook, Stephen Morris, and Bernard Sumner; Copyright: Zomba Music Publishing, Ltd.

"You Don't Bring Me Flowers," 1978: Words and music, Neil Diamond, Alan Bergman, and Marilyn Bergman; Copyright: Sony/ATV Music Publishing, Ltd.

"In the Air Tonight," 1981: Words and music, Phil Collins; Copyright: Hit and Run Music Publishing, Ltd.

"Brick," 1997: Words and music, Ben Folds and Darren Jesse; Copyright: Sony/ATV Music Publishing, Ltd.

"Ruby, Don't Take Your Love to Town," 1969: Words and music, Mel Tillis; Copyright: Universal Music Publishing, Ltd.

"All By Myself," 1976: Words and music, Eric Carmen; Copyright: Universal/Island Music, Ltd.

"Without You," 1970: Words and music, Pete Ham and Tom Evans; Copyright: Warner Chappell North America

"I Will Always Love You," 1974: Words and music, Dolly Parton; Copyright: Carlin Music Corp.

"Landslide," 1976: Words and music, Stevie Nicks; Copyright: Sony/ATV Music Publishing (UK)

"Send in the Clowns," 1975: Words and music, Stephen Sondheim; Copyright: Warner Chappell North America

"The River," 1980: Words and music, Bruce Springsteen; Copyright: Bruce Springsteen Zomba Music, Ltd.

"The Freshmen," 1997: Words and music, Brian Vander Ark. Copyright: Sid Flips Music/EMI April Music, Inc. (ASCAP)

"The Wreck of the Edmund Fitzgerald," 1976: Words and music, Gordon Lightfoot. Copyright: Moose Music, Ltd.

"Comfortably Numb," 1980: Words and music, Roger Waters and David Gilmour; Copyright: Pink Floyd Music Publishers, Ltd./Warner Chappell Artemis Music

"Maggie's Dream," 1984: Words and music, Dave Loggins and Lisa Silver; Copyright: Universal/MCA Music, Ltd.

"People Who Died," 1981: Words and music, Jim Carroll; Copyright: Hornall Bros Music, Ltd.

"Strange Fruit," 1939: Words by Lewis Allan (Abel Meeropol), arranged by Danny Mendelsohn; Copyright: Carlin Music Corp.

"DOA," 1971: Words and music, Jim Rutledge, Rick Cobb, Ed Grundy, Steve Hill, Lee Palmer, Nick Taylor; Copyright: Ledgefield Music (BMI)

"Sylvia's Mother," 1972: Words and music, Shel Silverstein; Copyright: Tro Essex Music, Ltd.

"The End," 1967: Words and music, Robby Krieger, Jim Morrison, Ray Manzarek, and John Densmore; Copyright: Render Music (London), Ltd.

"Alone Again (Naturally)," 1972: Words and music, Gilbert O'Sullivan; Sony/ATV Music Publishing, Ltd.

"Artificial Flowers," 1960: Words and music, Jerry Bock and Sheldon Harnick; Copyright: Carlin Music Corp.

"Indiana Wants Me," 1971: Words and music, R. Dean Taylor; Copyright: Jobete Music (UK) Ltd.

"Prayers for Rain," 1989: Words and music, Robert Smith, Simon Gallop, Roger O'Donnell, Porl Thompson, Lol Tolhurst, Boris Williams; Copyright: Fiction Songs, Ltd.

"Sister Morphine," 1969: Words by Marianne Faithful, music by Mick Jagger and Keith Richards; Copyright: Abkco Music Ltd./Omward Music, Ltd./Westminster Music, Ltd.

"Hurt," 1995: Words and music, Trent Reznor; Copyright: Universal/MCA Music, Ltd.

"Women's Prison," 2004: Words and music, Loretta Lynn; Copyright: Coal Mines Music, Inc.

"Seasons in the Sun," 1974: Music by Jacques Brel, Words by Rod McKuen; Copyright: Carlin Music Corp

"Total Eclipse of the Heart," 1983: Words and music, Jim Steinman; Copyright: EMI Virgin Music, Ltd.

"Honey," 1968: Words and music, Bobby Russell; Copyright: Peter Maurice Music Co., Ltd.

"The Shortest Story," 1976: Words and music, Harry Chapin; Copyright: Story Songs, Ltd.

"The Christmas Shoes," 2000: Words and music, Leonard Ahlstrom and Eddie Carswell; Copyright: Warner Chappell North America/Sony ATV Music Publishing